IMPROVISATION MADE EASIER

FRANK GAMBALE

**AN IMPROVISATION COURSE FOR
INTERMEDIATE TO ADVANCED GUITARISTS**

**COVER DESIGN: JORGE PAREDES
COVER PHOTOGRAPHS COURTESY OF MICHELLE MORTON
MUSIC TYPESETTING AND PAGE COMPOSITION BY CHELSEA MUSIC ENGRAVING**

D1601766

WARNER BROS. PUBLICATIONS - THE GLOBAL LEADER IN PRINT
USA: 15800 NW 48th Avenue, Miami, FL 33014

WARNER/CHAPPELL MUSIC

CANADA: 40 SHEPPARD AVE. WEST, SUITE 800
TORONTO, ONTARIO, M2N 6K9
SCANDINAVIA: P.O. BOX 533, VENDEVAGEN 85 B
S-182 15, DANDERYD, SWEDEN
AUSTRALIA: P.O. BOX 353
3 TALAVERA ROAD, NORTH RYDE N.S.W. 2113

Carisch
NUOVA CARISCH

ITALY: VIA CAMPANIA, 12
20098 S. GIULIANO MILANESE (MI)
ZONA INDUSTRIALE SESTO ULTERIANO
SPAIN: MAGALLANES, 25
28015 MADRID
FRANCE: 20, RUE DE LA VILLE-L'EVEQUE, 75008 PARIS

IMP
INTERNATIONAL MUSIC PUBLICATIONS LIMITED

ENGLAND: GRIFFIN HOUSE,
161 HAMMERSMITH ROAD, LONDON W6 8BS
GERMANY: MARSTALLSTR. 8, D-80539 MUNCHEN
DENMARK: DANMUSIK, VOGNMAGERGADE 7
DK 1120 KOBENHAVNK

Published by Manhattan Music, Inc.™

Distributed by Warner Bros. Publications
15800 N.W. 48th Avenue
Miami, FL 33014

TABLE OF CONTENTS

INTRODUCTION

Welcome to the *Frank Gambale Improvisation Made Easier* course. Over this twelve-chapter course we'll be looking in-depth at the twelve most important scale sounds you'll need to become a well-rounded guitarist. Of course we'll be looking not only at scales, but also at the chords and voicings derived from these scales, and licks that will keep you learning and challenged. I'll be presenting you with seven lessons per chapter. I'll be using only the keys of "E" and "A" throughout all of the examples. I believe that it is an unnecessary waste of time to learn everything in twelve keys on the guitar, mainly because every scale will look the same and incorporate the same fingerings. So "E" and "A" are sufficient to give you a good idea of how the scale shapes overlap on the guitar. At the end of each chord chapter there is a song study of all the information we'll have learned in the chapter. There's lots to learn, but take your time, there's no rush. This is a serious course here and I've attempted to make learning fun and easier. So, on that note (B♭), let's dive right in to Chapter 1, Lesson 1 — good luck.!

THE MIXOLYDIAN MODE
(D/E, E7sus, G/A...)

The mixolydian mode is built on the 5th note of a major scale. E mixolydian would have the same notes as the A major scale (A B C# D E F# G#) because E is the 5th scale degree of A. Therefore, E mixolydian is the notes of A major beginning on the note E: E F# G# A B C# D. An understanding of the intervallic relationship between each of these notes is necessary in order to understand the character of the mixolydian scale. To do that we must compare these notes to the standard scale from which all music theory is derived: THE MAJOR SCALE. If we compare E mixolydian to the notes of E major we have:

E Major:	E	F#	G#	A	B	C#	D#	E	F#	G#	A	B	C#
	1	2	3	4	5	6	7	8	9	10	11	12	13

E Mixolydian:	E	F#	G#	A	B	C#	**D**	E	F#	G#	A	B	C#
	1	2	3	4	5	6	♭**7**	8	9	10	11	12	13

Now you can see that the only difference is that the 7th degree is flat (lowered 1/2 step) in the mixolydian scale. By numbering the degrees we get a scale formula we can use which will be consistent with every mixolydian scale in every key.

Mixolydian:	1	2	3	4	5	6	♭7
		(9)		(11)		(13)	

You can see by this scale's interval content that the chords possible from mixolydian are dominant 7th chord characters: E7 (1 3 5 ♭7), E9 (1 3 5 ♭7 9), E11 or D/E (1 ♭7 9 11), and E13 (1 3 ♭7 13). These are just a few of the possibilities for chords available using the mixolydian interval structure: 1 2(9) 3 4(11) 5 6(13)♭7. The most popular mixolydian chord is undoubtedly the 11th chord, which is more commonly referred to as a major triad over a bass note which is one-whole-step higher. For E11, that would be the same as D/E (verbalized: "D over E"). Here, the D major triad is borrowing three notes from E mixolydian (D(♭7), F#(9) and A(11)) with the E below it functioning as the bass note or root of the chord. Visualizing this chord as a triad over a bass note makes it easier to find these chord voicings on the guitar. Now it's time to start putting all this information for mixolydian together.

Learn all seven scale fingerings for E mixolydian. Notice that the scales are written out, numbered in one-octave intervals: 1 2 3 4 5 6 ♭7. I think it's better for you to learn each scale by intervals rather than by the note names at first. The reason is that all the different keys would involve learning many different notes. But since the guitar shapes will remain the same for all keys, the relationship between all those notes remains the same — that is, the intervals from the root will always be 1 2 3 4 5 6 ♭7. Eventually it will be a good idea to learn the notes too, but for now just get familiar with the intervals. Practice these scale fingerings at a medium tempo. Remember, it's better to play accurately at a medium tempo than it is to play inaccurately at a fast tempo.

Fingering 1

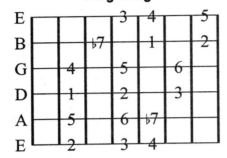

Fingering 2

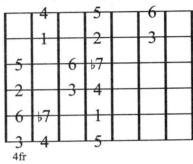

Fingering 3

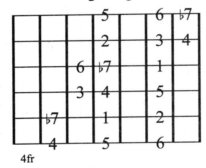

Fingering 4

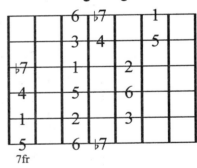

Fingering 5

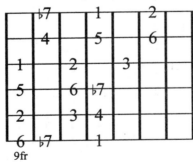

Fingering 6

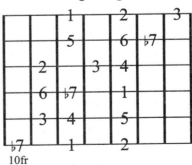

Fingering 7

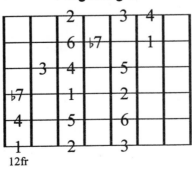

FRANK GAMBALE

Once again, I don't think it's necessary to learn all 12 keys, but to get used to key changes it's important to see how the scale fingerings overlap on the guitar. In Lesson two we'll learn the scale fingerings for A mixolydian. Once you've played all seven fingerings, combine Lessons 1 and 2 by playing the first fingering of E mixolydian, then the first fingering of A mixolydian, then the second fingering of E mixolydian, etc. This will help you get familiar with the concept of playing key changes in one fretboard location.

Fingering 1

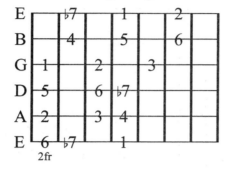

Fingering 2

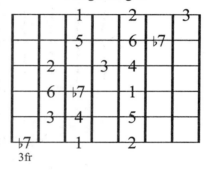

Fingering 3

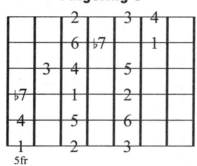

Fingering 4

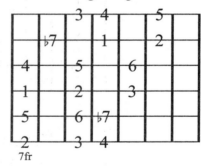

Fingering 5

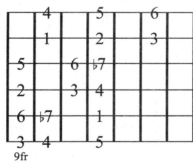

Fingering 6

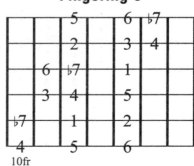

Fingering 7

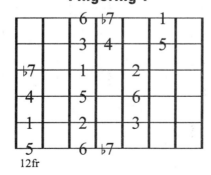

It is vital to have a strong chord vocabulary for soloing. Having lots of voicings for the D/E and G/A chords will certainly help. This is a particularly pleasing chord, as is the mixolydian scale over it, but we'll get to that a little later because now it's voicing time.

Learn these voicings thoroughly. Be able to grab them without missing a beat. Some of the voicings require a bit of a stretch; you may be able to use these voicings to warm up your hand muscles like a warm-up exercise.

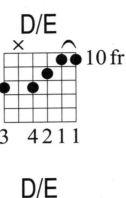

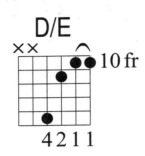

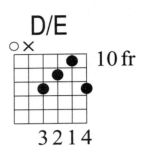

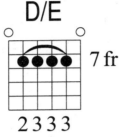

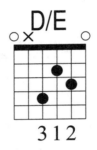

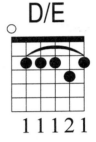

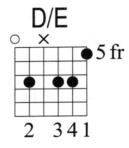

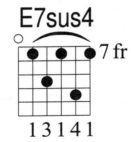

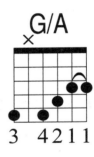

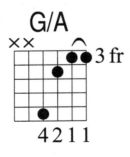

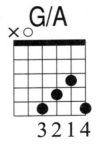

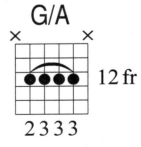

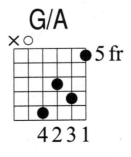

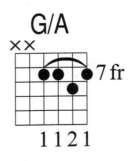

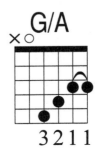

LICKS IN E MIXOLYDIAN

Now it's time to get some licks under your fingers. These licks will go from easy to hard and will be over the D/E chord. Remember, be patient. You can always slow any of the licks down or even stop them. Have fun!

Example 1

* Key signature denotes E mixolydian

Example 2

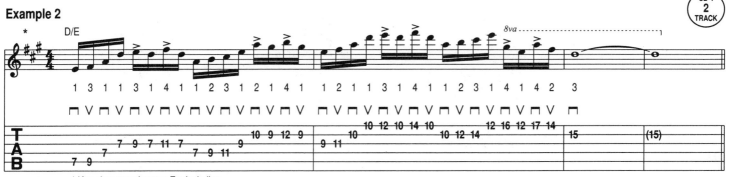

* Key signature denotes E mixolydian

Example 3

* Key signature denotes E mixolydian

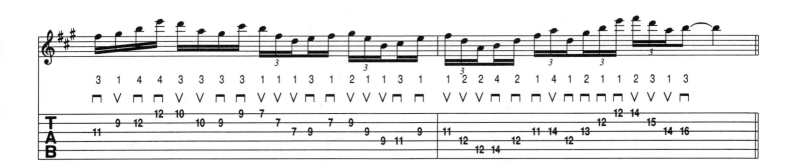

LICKS IN A MIXOLYDIAN

More licks, this time in A mixolydian. These licks will go from easy to hard and
will all be over the mixolydian G/A chord. Play them as accurately as possible and
at your own pace.

Example 4

* Key signature denotes A mixolydian

Example 5

* Key signature denotes A mixolydian

Example 6

* Key signature denotes A mixolydian

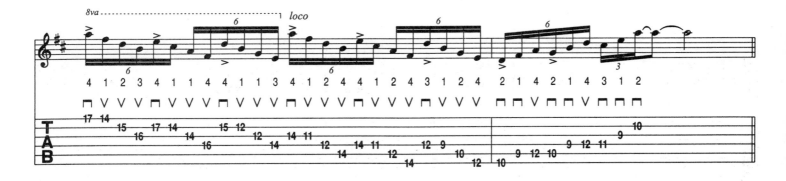

FRANK GAMBALE

Even more licks. This time we combine the two scales and chords. Study the notes carefully and try to get a feel for licks that have a smooth transition between keys through chord changes. THIS IS THE VERY ESSENCE OF IMPROVISING THROUGH CHANGES!

Example 7

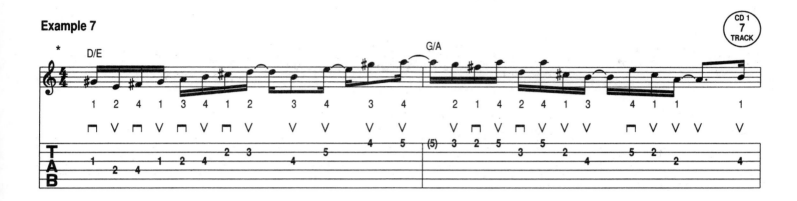

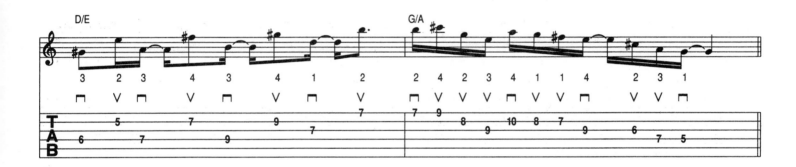

Example 8

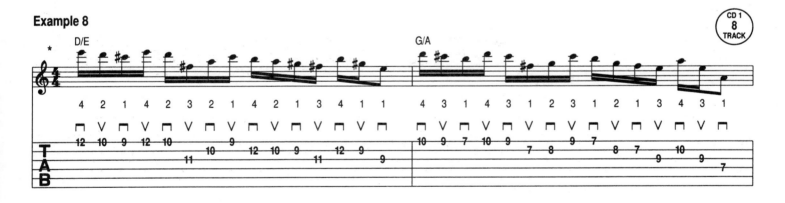

The last lesson in this first chapter will demonstrate the use of the 11th chord (usually indicated as a triad over a bass note, for example G/A) in a song context. Every chord will be an 11th chord so the corresponding scale for each chord will be mixolydian, relating to the chord's root. This way the melody will make perfect sense to you. I'll be using other keys as well as the two we've learned, but as I said before, it will be no problem because you already know the scale shapes from the earlier lessons. Enjoy the song.

Example 9

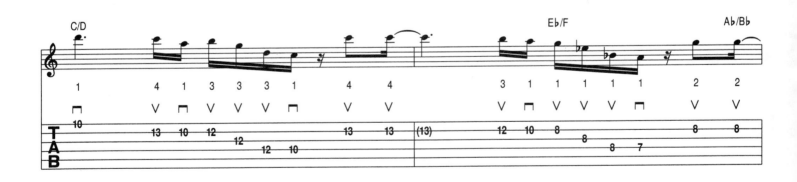

FRANK GAMBALE

CHAPTER 2

THE LYDIAN MODE
(F♯/E, Emaj7♯11, B/A...)

The lydian mode is built on the 4th note of a major scale. E lydian has the same notes as the B major scale (B C♯ D♯ E F♯ G♯ A♯) because E is the 4th scale degree of B. Therefore, E lydian is the notes of B major beginning on the note E: E F♯ G♯ A♯ B C♯ D♯. An understanding of the intervallic relationship between each of these notes is necessary in order to understand the character of the lydian scale. To do that we must compare these notes to the standard scale which all music theory is derived: THE MAJOR SCALE. If we compare E lydian to the notes of E major we have:

E Major:	E	F♯	G♯	A	B	C♯	D♯	E	F♯	G♯	A	B	C♯
	1	2	3	4	5	6	7	8	9	10	11	12	13

E Lydian:	E	F♯	G♯	**A♯**	B	C♯	D♯	E	F♯	G♯	**A♯**	B	C♯
	1	2	3	**♯4**	5	6	7	8	9	10	**♯11**	12	13

Now you can see that the only difference is that the 4th degree is sharp (raised 1/2 step) in the lydian scale. By numbering the degrees we get a scale formula we can use which will be consistent with every lydian scale in every key.

Lydian:	1	2	3	♯4	5	6	7
		(9)		(♯11)		(13)	

You can see by this scale's interval content that the chords that are possible from lydian are major chord characters: Emaj7 (1 3 5 7), Emaj9 (1 3 5 7 9), Emaj7♯11 (1 3 7 ♯11), and F♯/E (1 ♯4 6 9). These are just a few of the possibilities for chords available using the lydian interval structure: 1 – 2(9) – 3 – ♯4(♯11) – 5 – 6(13) – 7. The most popular lydian chord is undoubtedly the ⁶/₉♯11 chord, which is more commonly referred to as a major triad over a bass note which is one-whole-step lower. For E⁶/₉♯11), that would be the same as F♯/E (verbalized: "F♯ over E"). Here, the F♯ major triad is borrowing three notes from E lydian (F♯ = 9, A♯ = ♯11, C♯ = 6) with the E below it functioning as the bass note or root of the chord. Visualizing this chord as a triad over a bass note makes it easier to find these chord voicings on the guitar. Now it's time to start putting all this information for lydian together.

Learn all seven scale fingerings for E lydian. Notice that the scales are written out, numbered in one-octave intervals: 1 2 3 #4 5 6 7. Practice these scale fingerings at a medium tempo. Remember, it's better to play it accurately at a medium tempo than it is to play inaccurately at a fast tempo.

Fingering 1

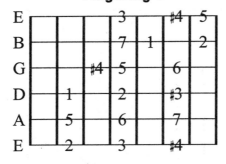

Fingering 2

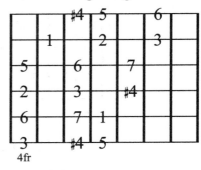

Fingering 3

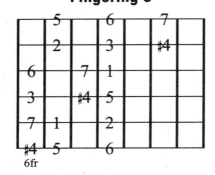

Fingering 4

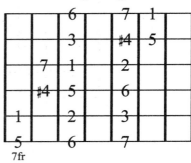

Fingering 5

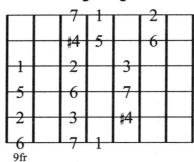

Fingering 6

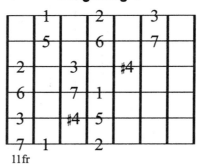

Fingering 7

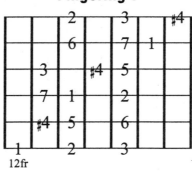

SCALE FINGERINGS FOR A LYDIAN

Once again, I don't think it's necessary to learn all 12 keys, but to get you used to key changes it's important to see how the scale fingerings overlap on the guitar, so in this lesson we'll learn the scale fingerings for A lydian. Once you've played all seven fingerings for A lydian, combine Lessons 1 and 2 by playing the first fingering of E lydian, then the first fingering of A lydian, then the second fingering of E lydian, etc. This will help you get familiar with the concept of playing key changes in one fretboard location.

Fingering 1

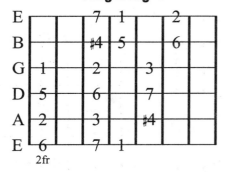

Fingering 2

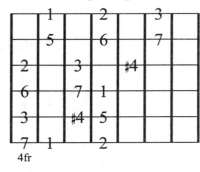

Fingering 3

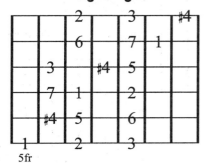

Fingering 4

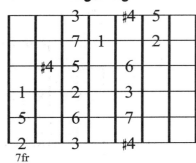

Fingering 5

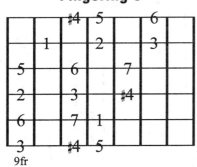

Fingering 6

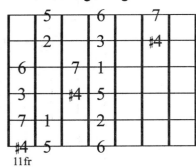

Fingering 7

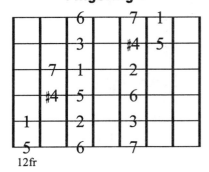

It is vital to have a strong chord vocabulary. Having lots of voicings for the F♯/E and B/A chords will certainly help. This is a particularly pleasing chord, as is the lydian scale over it. Learn these voicings thoroughly. Be able to grab them without missing a beat.

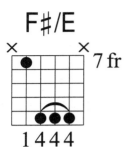

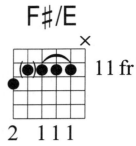

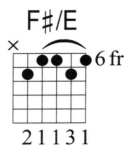

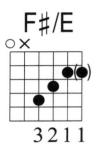

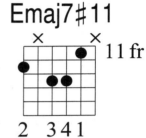

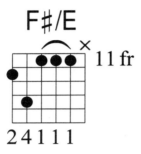

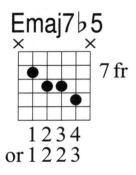

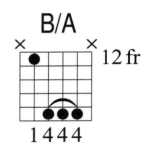

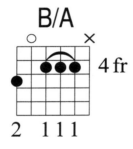

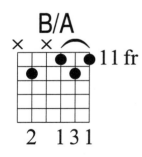

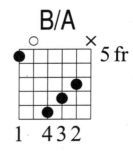

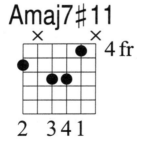

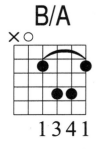

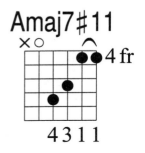

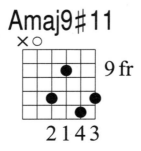

LICKS IN E LYDIAN

Now it's time again to get some licks under your fingers. These licks will go from easy to hard and will be over the F#/E chord. Remember, be patient. You can always slow any of the licks down or even stop them. Have fun!

Example 10

* Key signature denotes E lydian

Example 11

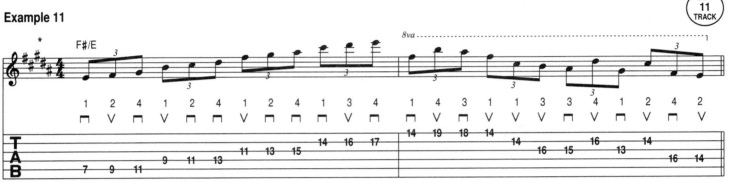

* Key signature denotes E lydian

Example 12

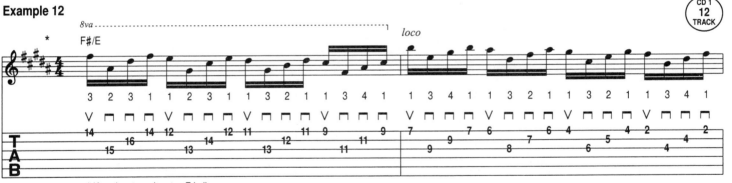

* Key signature denotes E lydian

More licks, this time in A lydian. These licks will go from easy to hard and will all be over the lydian B/A chord. Play them as accurately as possible and at your own pace.

Example 13

* Key signature denotes A lydian

Example 14

* Key signature denotes A lydian

Example 15

* Key signature denotes A lydian

FRANK GAMBALE

COMBINATION LICKS IN E AND A LYDIAN

Even more licks. This time we combine the two scales and chords. Study the notes carefully and try to get a feel for licks that have a smooth transition between keys through chord changes.

Example 16

Example 17

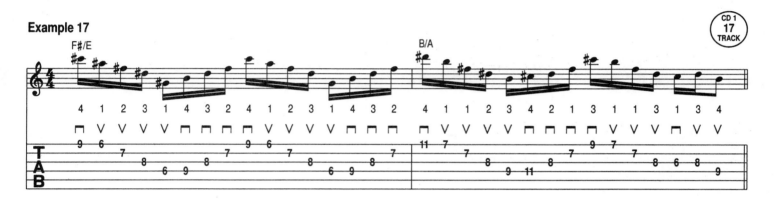

Example 18

This lesson will demonstrate the use of the lydian chord in a song context. Every chord will be a lydian chord, so the corresponding scale for each chord will be lydian, relating to the chord's root. This way the melody will make perfect sense to you. I'll be using other keys as well as the two we've learned, but as I said before, it will be no problem because you already know the scale shapes from the earlier lessons. Enjoy the song.

Example 19

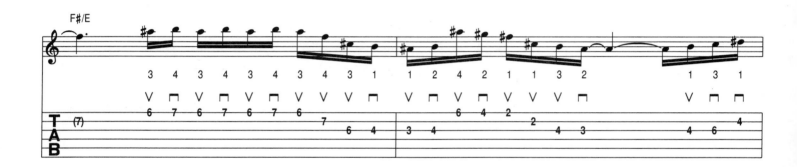

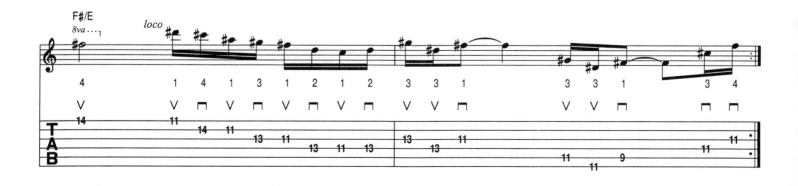

FRANK GAMBALE

CHAPTER 3

THE DORIAN MODE
(Emin7, Emin9, Emin11...)

The dorian mode is built on the 2nd note of a major scale. E dorian would have the same notes as the D major scale (D E F♯ G A B C♯) because E is the 2nd scale degree of D. Therefore, E dorian is the notes of D major beginning on the note E = E F♯ G A B C♯ D (E dorian). An understanding of the intervallic relationship between these notes is necessary in order to understand the character of the dorian scale. To do that we must compare these notes to the standard scale which all music theory is derived: THE MAJOR SCALE. If we compare E dorian to the notes of E major we have:

E Major:	E	F♯	G♯	A	B	C♯	D♯	F♯	E	G♯	A	B	C♯
	1	2	3	4	5	6	7	8	9	10	11	12	13

E Dorian:	E	F♯	**G**	A	B	C♯	**D**	E	F♯	**G**	A	B	C♯
	1	2	♭**3**	4	5	6	♭**7**	8	9	♭**10**	11	12	13

Now you can see that the only difference is that the 3rd and 7th degrees are flat (lowered 1/2 step) in the dorian scale. By numbering the degrees we get a scale formula we can use which will be consistent with every dorian scale in every key.

Dorian:	1	2	♭3	4	5	6	♭7
		(9)		(11)		(13)	

You can see by this scale's interval content that the chords possible from dorian are minor chord characters: Emin7 (1 ♭3 5 ♭7), Emin9 (1 ♭3 5 ♭7 9), and Emin11 (1 ♭3 ♭7 11). These are just a few of the possibilities for chords available using the dorian interval structure: 1 2(9) ♭3 4(11) 5 6(13) ♭7. The most popular dorian chord is undoubtedly the minor 7 chord.

Learn all seven scale fingerings for E dorian. Notice that the scales are written out, numbered in one-octave intervals: 1 2 ♭3 4 5 6 ♭7. Practice these scale fingerings at a medium tempo. Remember, it's better to play it accurately at a medium tempo than it is to play inaccurately at a fast tempo.

Fingering 1

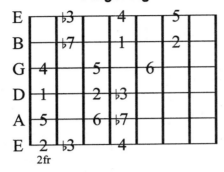

Fingering 2

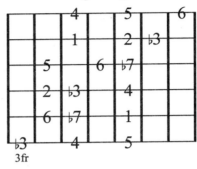

Fingering 3

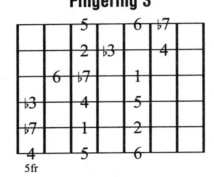

Fingering 4

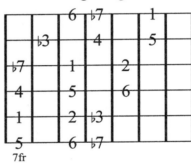

Fingering 5

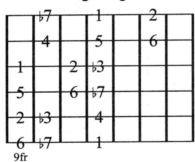

Fingering 6

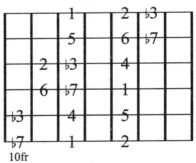

Fingering 7

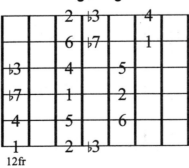

Once again, I don't think it's necessary to learn all 12 keys. Once you've played all seven fingerings for A dorian, combine Lessons 1 and 2 by playing the first fingering of E dorian, then the first fingering of A dorian, then the second fingering of E dorian, etc.

Fingering 1

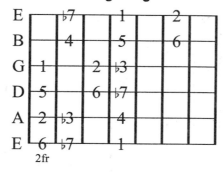

Fingering 2

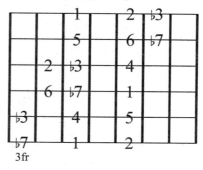

Fingering 3

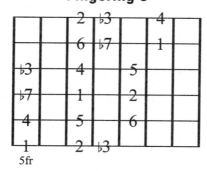

Fingering 4

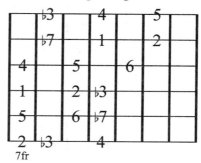

Fingering 5

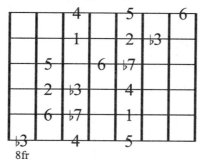

Fingering 6

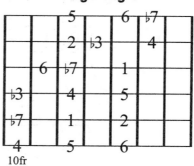

Fingering 7

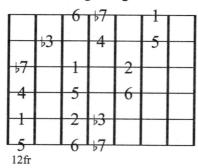

It is vital to have a strong chord vocabulary. Having lots of voicings for the Em7 and Am7 chords will be useful. Learn these voicings thoroughly. Be able to grab them without missing a beat.

Emin7

4 3 2 1 1

Emin7
1 3 2 2

Emin11
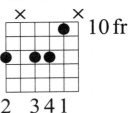
10 fr
2 3 4 1

Emin9
8 fr
2 4 1 3

Emin7
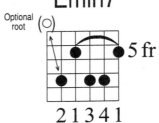
Optional root
5 fr
2 1 3 4 1

Emin11
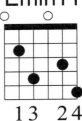
1 3 2 4

Emin13
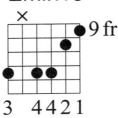
9 fr
3   4 4 2 1

Emin9
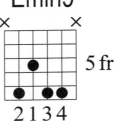
5 fr
2 1 3 4

Amin7
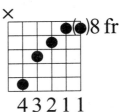
8 fr
4 3 2 1 1

Amin9
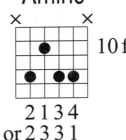
10 fr
2 1 3 4
or 2 3 3 1

Amin11
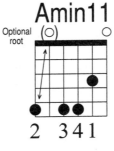
Optional root
2 3 4 1

Amin9
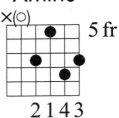
5 fr
2 1 4 3

Amin11
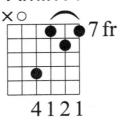
7 fr
4 1 2 1

Amin13
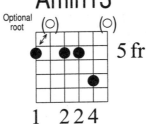
Optional root
5 fr
1 2 2 4

Amin7
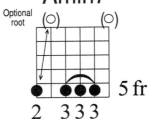
Optional root
5 fr
2 3 3 3

Now it's time again to get some licks under your fingers. These licks will go from easy to hard and will be over the Em7 chord. Remember, be patient. You can always slow any of the licks down or even stop them. Have fun!

Example 20

* Key signature denotes E dorian

Example 21

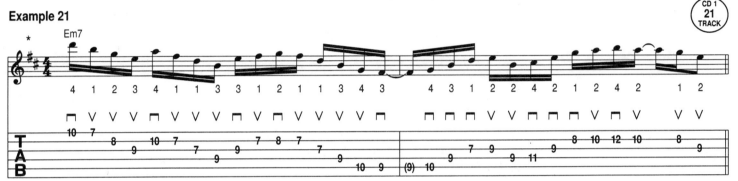

* Key signature denotes E dorian

Example 22

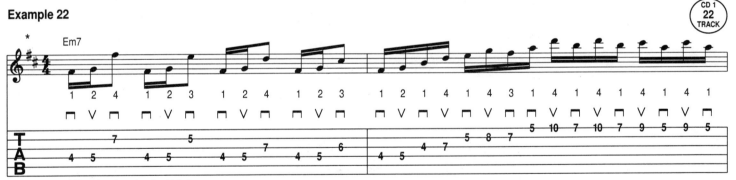

* Key signature denotes E dorian

More licks, this time in A dorian. These licks will go from easy to hard and will all be over the Am7 chord. Play them as accurately as possible and at your own pace.

Example 23

* Key signature denotes A dorian

Example 24

* Key signature denotes A dorian

Example 25

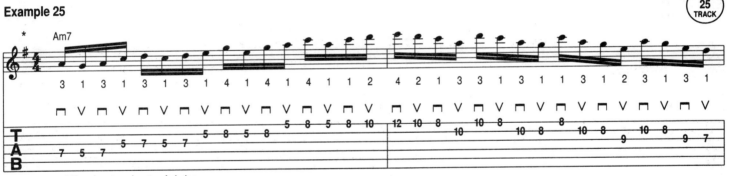

* Key signature denotes A dorian

FRANK GAMBALE

Even more licks. This time we combine the two scales and chords. Study the notes carefully and try to get a feel for licks that have a smooth transition between keys through chord changes.

Example 26

Example 27

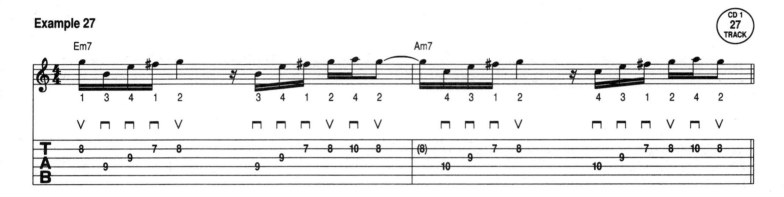

Example 28

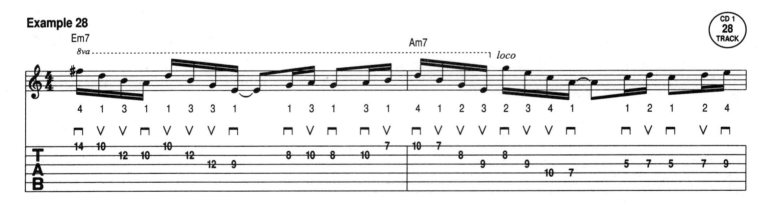

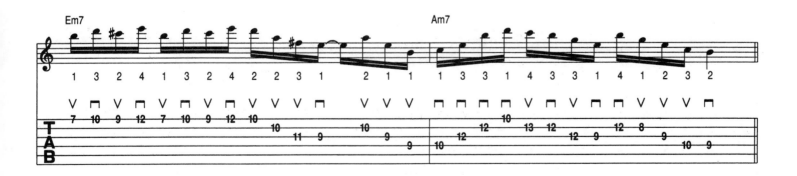

This lesson will demonstrate the use of the dorian chord in a song context. Every chord will be a dorian chord. Enjoy the song.

Example 29

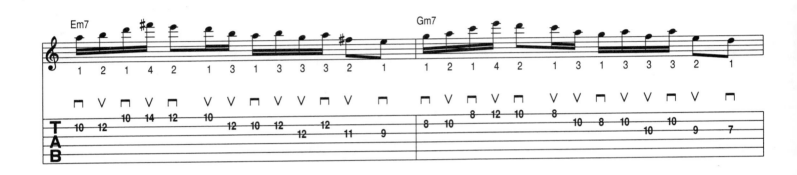

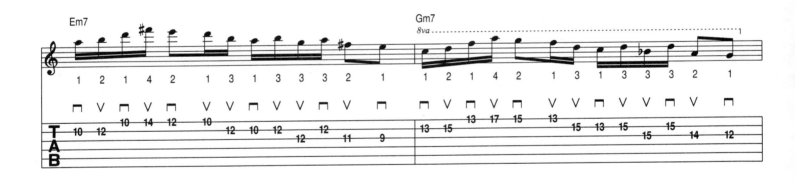

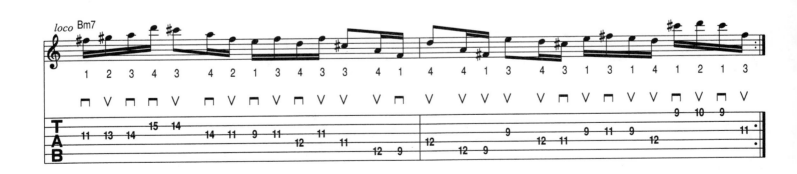

FRANK GAMBALE

CHAPTER 4

THE IONIAN MODE (Emaj7, E(9)...)

E major would obviously have the same notes as the E major scale. Therefore, the notes of E major are: E F♯ G♯ A B C♯ D♯. The intervallic relationship between each of these notes reveals the character of the major scale.

E Major:	E	F♯	G♯	A	B	C♯	D♯	E	F♯	G♯	A	B	C♯
	1	2	3	4	5	6	7	8	9	10	11	12	13

By numbering the degrees we get a scale formula we can use which will be consistent with every major scale in every key.

Ionian:	1	2	3	4	5	6	7
		(9)		(11)		(13)	

You can see by this scale's interval content that the chords possible from major are major chord characters: Emaj7 (1 3 5 7), E(add9) (1 3 5 9), Emaj9 (1 3 5 7 9), and Emaj13 (1 3 7 13). These are just a few of the possibilities for chords available using the major interval structure: 1   2(9)   3   4(11)   5   6(13)   7. The most popular major chords are undoubtedly the major 7 chord and the major(add9).

Learn all seven scale fingerings for the E major scale. Once again the scales are written out, numbered in one-octave intervals: 1 2 3 4 5 6 7. Practice these scale fingerings at a medium tempo.

Fingering 1

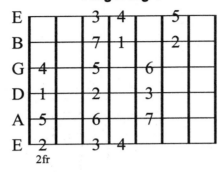

Fingering 2

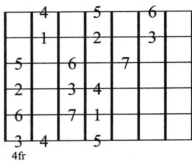

Fingering 3

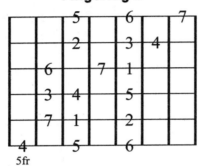

Fingering 4

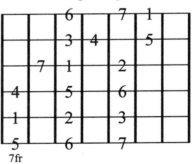

Fingering 5

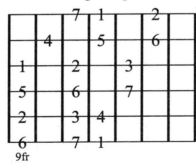

Fingering 6

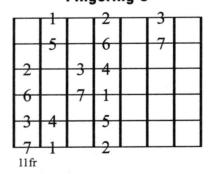

Fingering 7

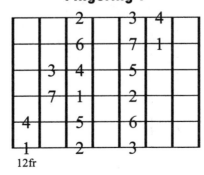

In this lesson we'll learn the scale fingerings for A major. Once you've played all seven fingerings for A major, combine Lessons 1 and 2 by playing the first fingering of E major, then the first fingering of A major, then the second fingering of E major, etc.

Fingering 1

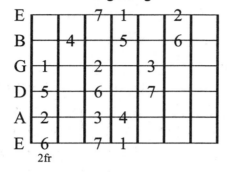

Fingering 2

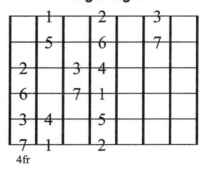

Fingering 3

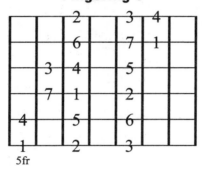

Fingering 4

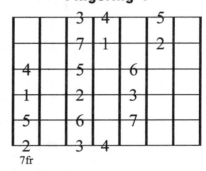

Fingering 5

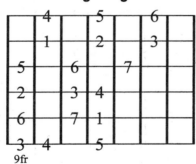

Fingering 6

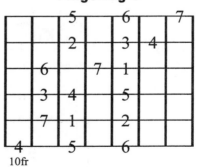

Fingering 7

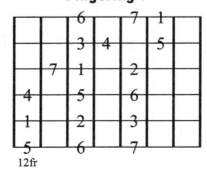

Now it's time to look at the most useful voicings derived from the major scale. It will be mostly major 7 chords and some other variations. Have fun!

Emaj7
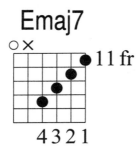
4 3 2 1

Emaj7
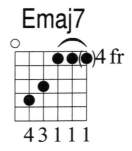
4 3 1 1 1

Emaj7
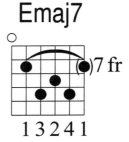
1 3 2 4 1

Emaj9
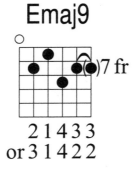
2 1 4 3 3
or 3 1 4 2 2

Emaj9
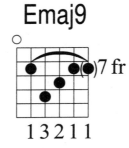
1 3 2 1 1

E(9)
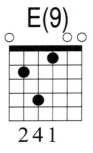
2 4 1

E(9)
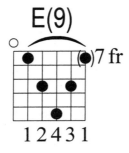
1 2 4 3 1

E(9)
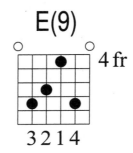
3 2 1 4

E(9)
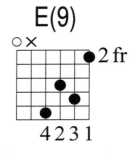
4 2 3 1

Emaj7
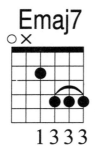
1 3 3 3

Amaj7
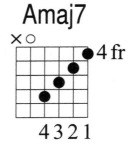
4 3 2 1

Amaj9
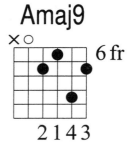
2 1 4 3

A(9)
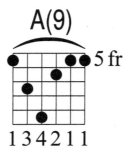
1 3 4 2 1 1

A(9)
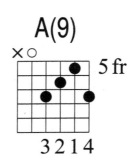
3 2 1 4

A(9)
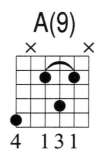
4   1 3 1

Now it's time again to get some more licks under your fingers. These licks will go from easy to hard and will be over the Emaj7 and E(9) chords. Remember, have fun!

Example 30

Example 31

Example 32

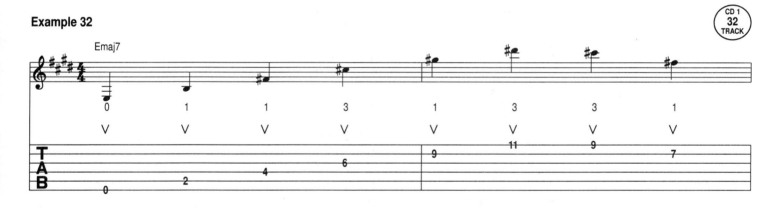

More licks, this time in A major. These licks will go from easy to hard and will all be over the Amaj7 chord. Play them as accurately as possible and at your own pace.

Example 33

Example 34

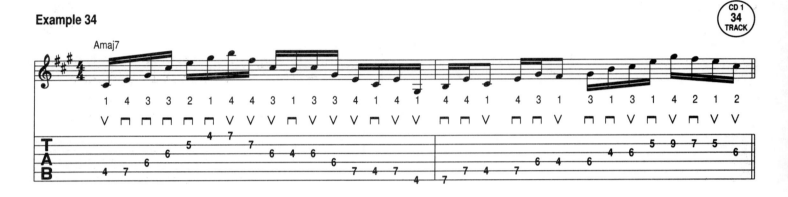

Example 35

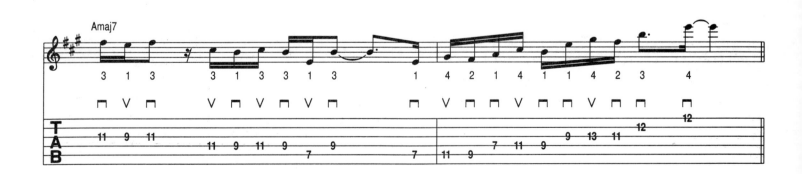

Even more licks. This time we combine the two scales and chords. Study the notes carefully and try to get a feel for licks that have a smooth transition between keys through chord changes.

Example 36

Example 37

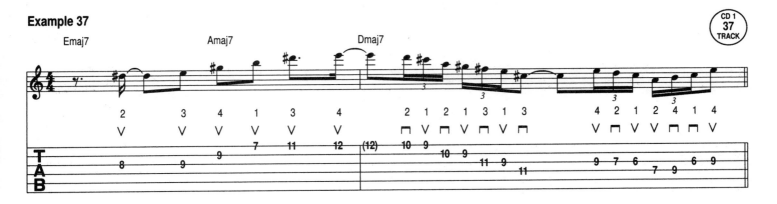

Example 38

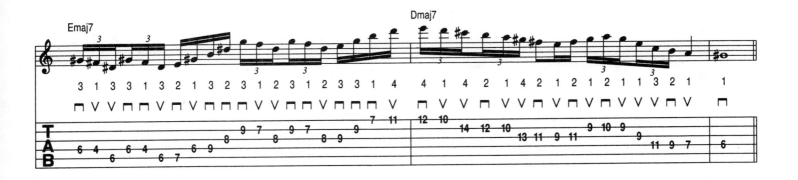

SONG EXAMPLE USING THE MAJOR 7 CHORD

This lesson will demonstrate the use of the major chord in a song context. Every chord will be a major-type chord so the corresponding scale for each chord will be major, relating to the chord's root. This way the melody will make perfect sense to you. Enjoy the song.

Example 39

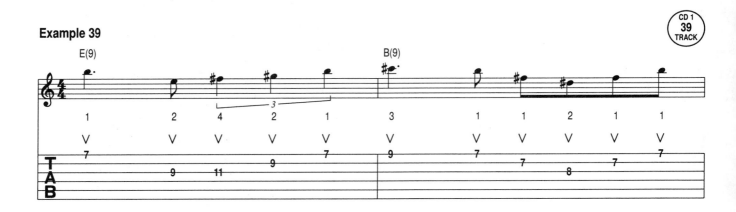

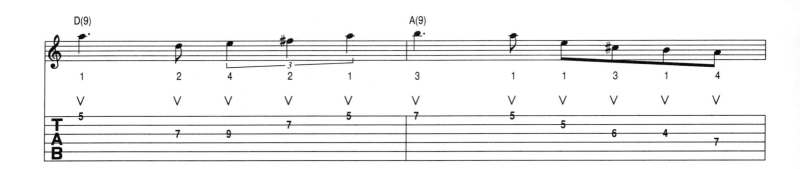

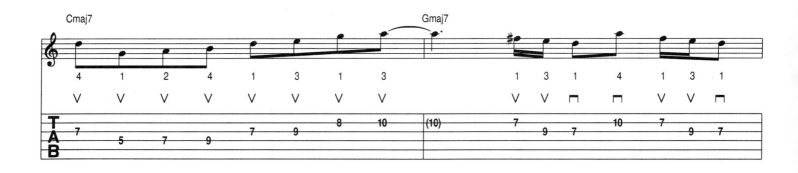

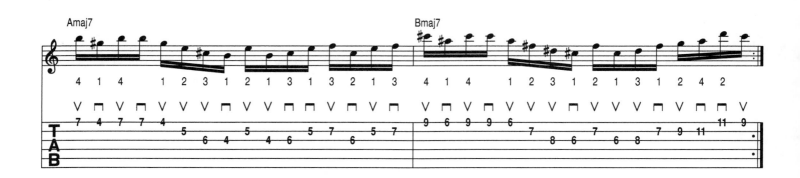

FRANK GAMBALE

CHAPTER 5

THE LOCRIAN MODE
(Emin7♭5, B♭maj7♭5/E...)

The locrian mode is built on the 7th note of a major scale. E locrian would have the same notes as the F major scale (F G A B♭ C D E) because E is the 7th scale degree of F. Therefore, E locrian is the notes of F major beginning on the note E: E F G A B♭ C D. An understanding of the intervallic relationship between these notes is necessary in order to understand the character of the locrian scale. To do that we must compare these notes to the major scale. If we compare E locrian to the notes of E major we have:

E Major:	E	F#	G#	A	B	C#	D#	E	F#	G#	A	B	C#
	1	2	3	4	5	6	7	8	9	10	11	12	13

E Locrian:	E	**F**	**G**	A	**B♭**	**C**	**D**	E	**F**	**G**	A	**B♭**	**C**
	1	♭**2**	♭**3**	4	♭**5**	♭**6**	♭**7**	8	♭**9**	♭**10**	11	♭**12**	♭**13**

Now you can see that the differences are that the 2nd, 3rd, 5th, 6th, and 7th degrees are flat (lowered 1/2 step) in the locrian scale. By numbering the degrees we get a scale formula we can use which will be consistent with every locrian scale in every key.

Locrian:	1	♭2	♭3	4	♭5	♭6	♭7
		(♭9)		(11)		(♭13)	

You can see by this scale's interval content that the chords possible from locrian are minor chord characters: Emin7♭5 (1 ♭3 ♭5 ♭7) and Emin11 (1 ♭3 ♭7 11). These are just a few of the possibilities for chords available using the locrian interval structure: 1 ♭2(♭9) ♭3 4(11) ♭5 ♭6(♭13) ♭7. The most popular locrian chord is undoubtedly the minor 7(♭5) chord.

Learn all seven scale fingerings for E locrian. Notice that the scales are written out, numbered in one-octave intervals: 1 ♭2 ♭3 4 ♭5 ♭6 ♭7. Practice these scale fingerings at a medium tempo.

Fingering 1

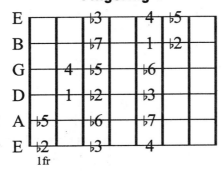

Fingering 2

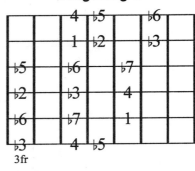

Fingering 3

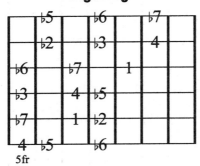

Fingering 4

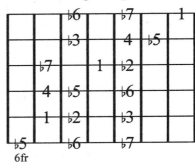

Fingering 5

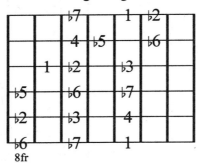

Fingering 6

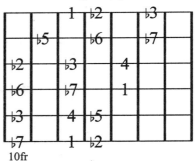

Fingering 7

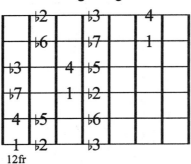

Once you've played all seven fingerings for A locrian, combine Lessons 1 and 2 by playing the first fingering of E locrian, then the first fingering of A locrian, then the second fingering of E locrian, etc.

Fingering 1

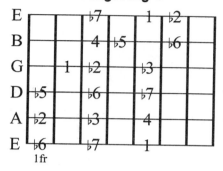

Fingering 2

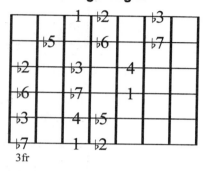

Fingering 3

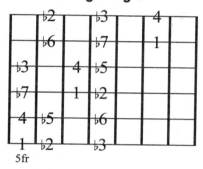

Fingering 4

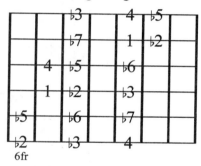

Fingering 5

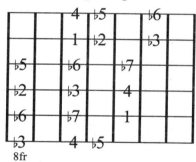

Fingering 6

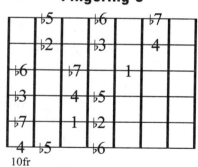

Fingering 7

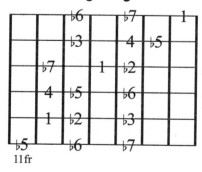

Having lots of voicings for the Emin7♭5 and Amin7♭5 chords will be useful. Learn these voicings thoroughly. Be able to grab them quickly.

Emin7♭5

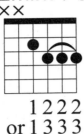

1 2 2 2
or 1 3 3 3

Emin7♭5

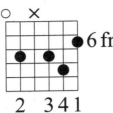

6 fr

2 3 4 1

B♭/E

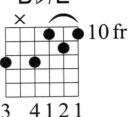

10 fr

3 4 1 2 1

Emin7♭5

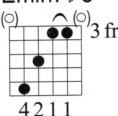

3 fr

4 2 1 1

Emin7♭5

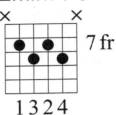

7 fr

1 3 2 4

B♭/E

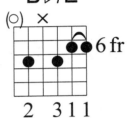

6 fr

2 3 1 1

B♭maj7♭5/E

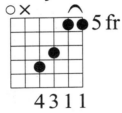

5 fr

4 3 1 1

Amin7♭5

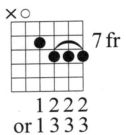

7 fr

1 2 2 2
or 1 3 3 3

Amin7♭5

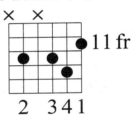

11 fr

2 3 4 1

E♭/A

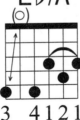

3 4 1 2 1

Amin7♭5

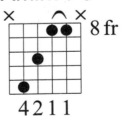

8 fr

4 2 1 1

Amin7♭5

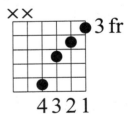

3 fr

4 3 2 1

Amin7♭5

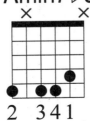

2 3 4 1

E♭/A

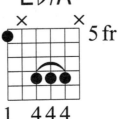

5 fr

1 4 4 4

E♭/A

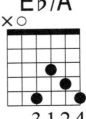

3 1 2 4

Now it's time again to get some more licks under your fingers. Once again the licks will go from easy to hard and will be over the Emin7b5 chord. Remember, have fun!

Example 40

* Key signature denotes E locrian

Example 41

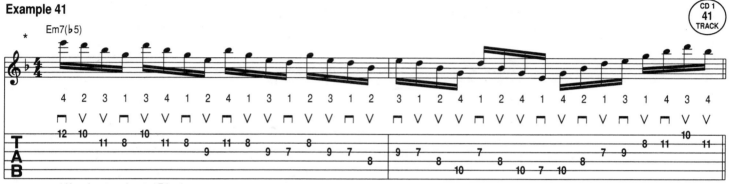

* Key signature denotes E locrian

Example 42

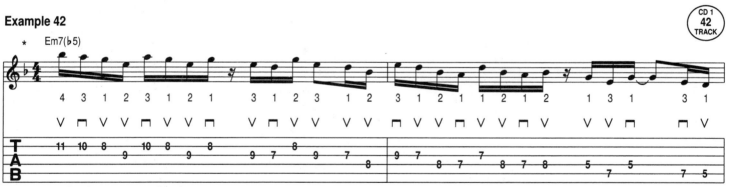

* Key signature denotes E locrian

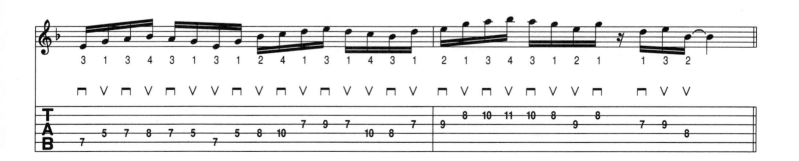

LICKS IN A LOCRIAN

More licks, this time in A locrian. These licks will go from easy to hard and will all be over the Amin7♭5 chord. Play them as accurately as possible.

Example 43

* Key signature denotes A locrian

Example 44

* Key signature denotes A locrian

Example 45

* Key signature denotes A locrian

FRANK GAMBALE

Even more licks. This time we combine the two scales and chords. Study the notes carefully and try to get a feel for licks that have a smooth transition between keys through chord changes.

Example 46

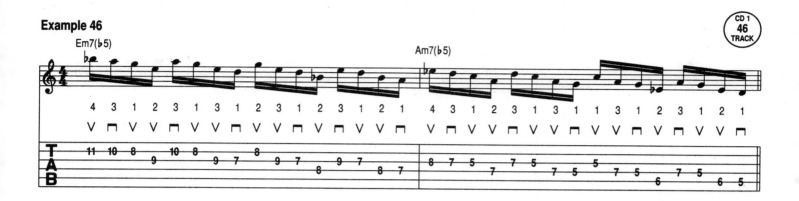

Example 47

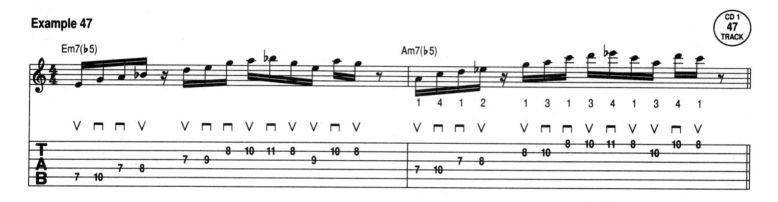

Example 48

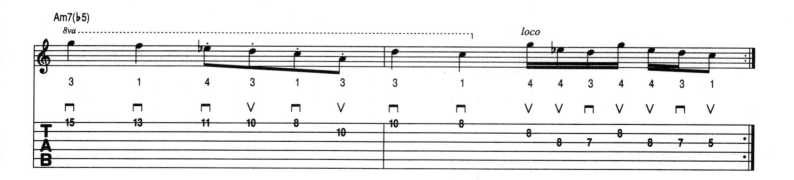

This lesson will demonstrate the use of the locrian chord in a song context. I will also use some other chord types to make the example more musical and realistic. Enjoy!

Example 49

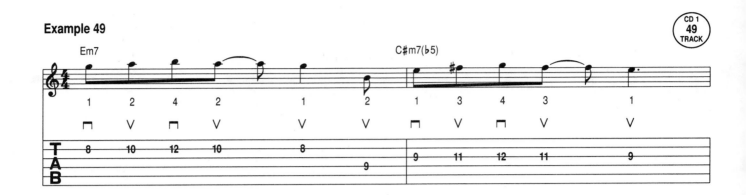

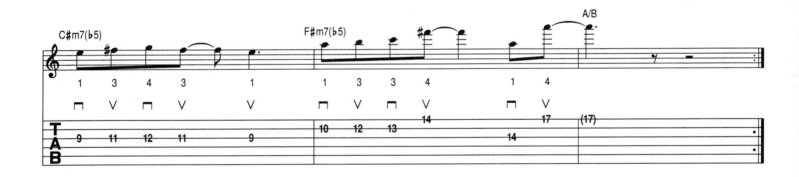

CHAPTER 6

THE PHRYGIAN MODE
(Fmaj7♭5/E, F/E, E5♭9, B°/E...)

The phrygian mode is built on the 3rd note of a major scale. E phrygian would have the same notes as the C major scale (C D E F G A B) because E is the 3rd scale degree of C. Therefore, E phrygian is the notes of C major beginning on the note E: E F G A B C D. An understanding of the intervallic relationship between these notes is necessary in order to understand the character of the phrygian scale. To do that we must compare these notes to the major scale. If we compare E phrygian to the notes of E major we have:

E Major:	E	F♯	G♯	A	B	C♯	D♯	E	F♯	G♯	A	B	C♯
	1	2	3	4	5	6	7	8	9	10	11	12	13

E Phrygian:	E	**F**	**G**	A	B	**C**	**D**	E	**F**	**G**	A	B	**C**
	1	♭**2**	♭**3**	4	5	♭**6**	♭**7**	8	♭**9**	♭**10**	11	12	♭**13**

Now you can see that the differences are that the 2nd, 3rd, 6th, and 7th degrees are flat (lowered 1/2 step) in the phrygian scale. By numbering the degrees we get a scale formula we can use which will be consistent with every phrygian scale in every key.

Phrygian:	1	♭2	♭3	4	5	♭6	♭7
		(♭9)		(11)		(♭13)	

You can see by this scale's interval content that the chords possible from phrygian are minor chord characters: Emin♭9 (1 ♭3 5 ♭9) and Fmaj7♭5/E (1 4 5 ♭9). These are just a few of the possibilities for chords available using the phrygian interval structure: 1 ♭2(♭9) ♭3 4(11) 5 ♭6(♭13) ♭7. The most popular E phrygian chord is undoubtedly the Fmaj7♭5/E chord.

Learn all seven scale fingerings for E phrygian. Notice that the scales are written out, numbered in one-octave intervals: 1 ♭2 ♭3 4 5 ♭6 ♭7. Practice these scale fingerings at a medium tempo.

Fingering 1

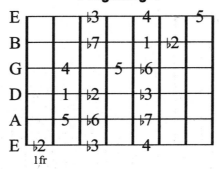

Fingering 2

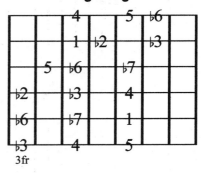

Fingering 3

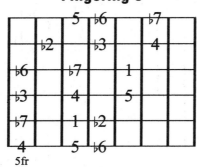

Fingering 4

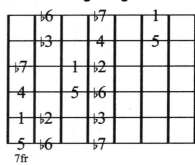

Fingering 5

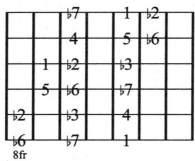

Fingering 6

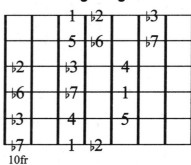

Fingering 7

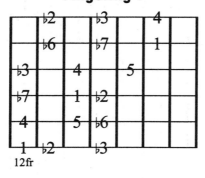

SCALE FINGERINGS FOR A PHRYGIAN

Once you've played all seven fingerings for A phrygian, combine Lessons 1 and 2 by playing the first fingering of E phrygian, then the first fingering of A phrygian, then the second fingering of E phrygian, etc.

Fingering 1
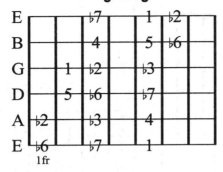

Fingering 2
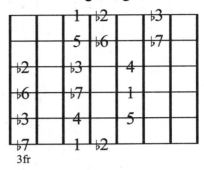

Fingering 3
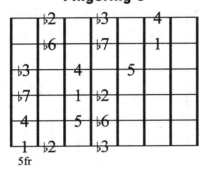

Fingering 4
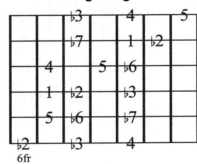

Fingering 5
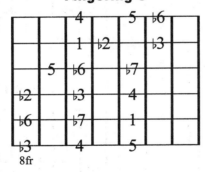

Fingering 6
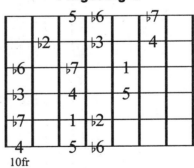

Fingering 7
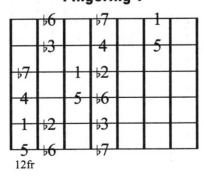

Here are some voicings for the Fmaj7#11/E, Bbmaj7#11/A, and other chords available to us from the intervals unique to the phrygian scale.

F/E

Dmin⁶/₉/E

E5b9
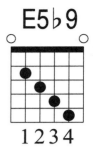

E5b9

Fmaj7b5/E
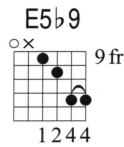

Fmaj7b5/E
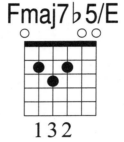

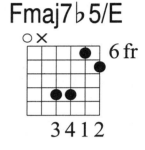

B°/E

Bb/A

Gmin⁶/₉/A
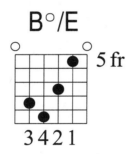

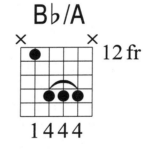

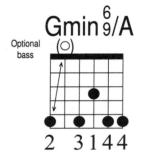

Bb/A

Bbmaj7/A

Bbmaj7b5/A
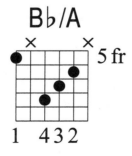

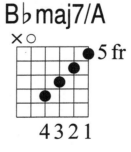

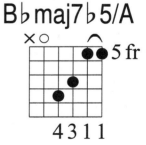

E°/A

C13/A

Gmin(add9)/A
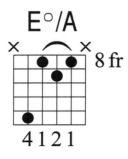

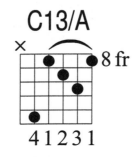

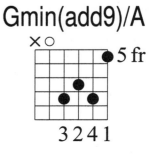

Now it's time again to get some more licks under your fingers. Once again the licks will go from easy to hard and will be over the Fmaj7#11/E chord. Have fun!

Example 50

* Fmaj7(♭5)/E

* Key signature denotes E phrygian

Example 51

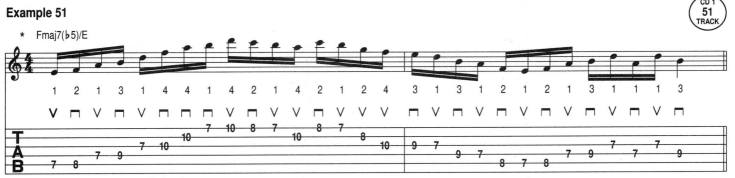

* Fmaj7(♭5)/E

* Key signature denotes E phrygian

Example 52

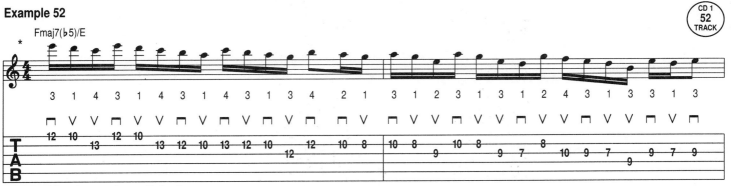

Fmaj7(♭5)/E

* Key signature denotes E phrygian

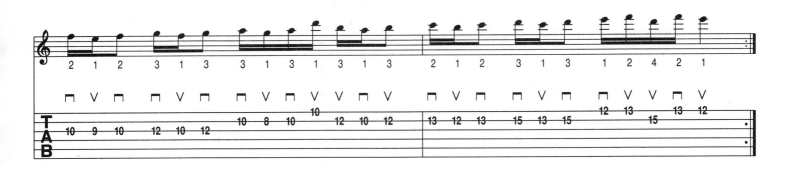

More licks, this time in A phrygian. These licks will go from easy to hard and will all be over the Bbmaj7#11/A chord. Play them as accurately as possible.

Example 53

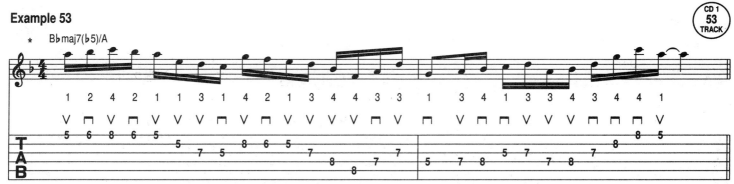

* Key signature denotes A phrygian

Example 54

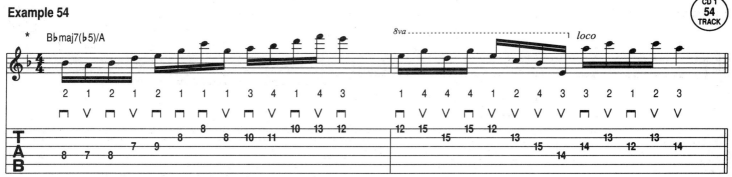

* Key signature denotes A phrygian

Example 55

* Key signature denotes A phrygian

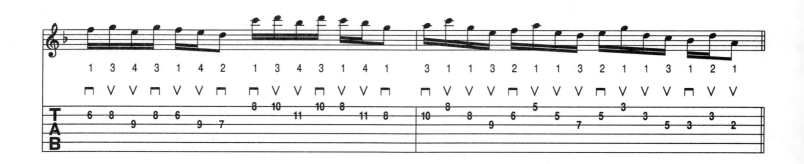

More licks. This time we combine the two scales and chords. Study the notes carefully, being sure to read the notes accurately. Good luck!

Example 56

Example 57

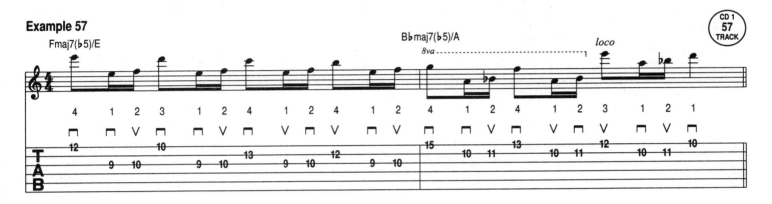

Example 58

This lesson will demonstrate the use of the phrygian chord in a song context. I've decided to use only the chords we've learned so far in this musical example. Have fun!

Example 59

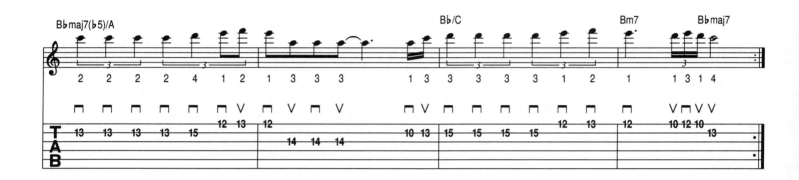

FRANK GAMBALE

CHAPTER 7

THE AEOLIAN MODE
(Emin7♯5, Emin11♯5, Fmaj7/A...)

The aeolian mode is built on the 6th note of a major scale. E aeolian would have the same notes as the G major scale (G A B C D E F♯) because E is the 6th scale degree of G. Therefore, E aeolian is the notes of G major beginning on the note E: E F♯ G A B C D. An understanding of the intervallic relationship between these notes is necessary in order to understand the character of the aeolian scale. To do that we must compare these notes to the major scale. If we compare E aeolian to the notes of E major we have:

E Major:

E	F♯	G♯	A	B	C♯	D♯	E	F♯	G♯	A	B	C♯
1	2	3	4	5	6	7	8	9	10	11	12	13

E Aeolian:

E	F♯	**G**	A	B	**C**	**D**	E	F♯	**G**	A	B	**C**
1	2	♭**3**	4	5	♭**6**	♭**7**	8	9	♭**10**	11	12	♭**13**

Now you can see that the differences are that the 3rd, 6th, and 7th degrees are flat (lowered 1/2 step) in the aeolian scale. By numbering the degrees we get a scale formula we can use which will be consistent with every aeolian scale in every key.

Aeolian:

1	2	♭3	4	5	♭6	♭7
	(9)		(11)		(♭13)	

You can see by this scale's interval content that the chords possible from aeolian are minor chord characters: Emin7♯5 (1 ♭3 ♯5 ♭7). This is just one of the possibilities for chords available using the aeolian interval structure: 1   2(9)   ♭3   4(11)   5   ♭6(♭13)   ♭7. The most popular aeolian chord is undoubtedly the minor 7(♯5) chord.

Learn all seven scale fingerings for E aeolian. Notice that the scales are written out, numbered in one-octave intervals: 1 2 ♭3 4 5 ♭6 ♭7. Practice these scale fingerings at a medium tempo.

Fingering 1

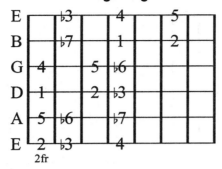

Fingering 2

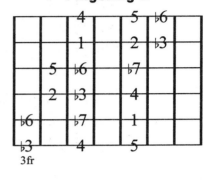

Fingering 3

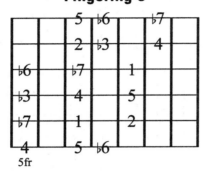

Fingering 4

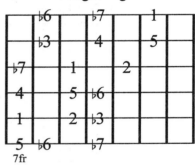

Fingering 5

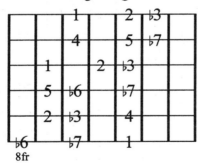

Fingering 6

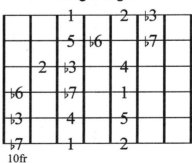

Fingering 7

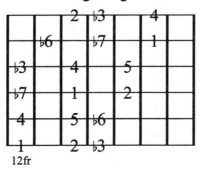

Once you've played all seven fingerings for A aeolian, combine Lessons 1 and 2 by playing the first fingering of E aeolian, then the first fingering of A aeolian, then the second fingering of E aeolian, etc.

Fingering 1

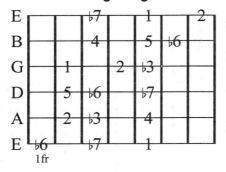

Fingering 3

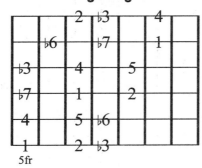

Fingering 5

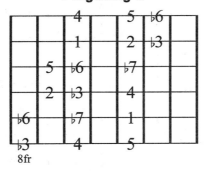

Fingering 7

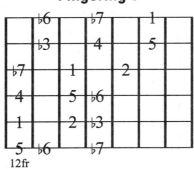

Fingering 2

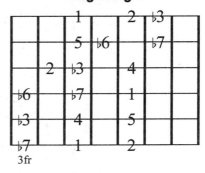

Fingering 4

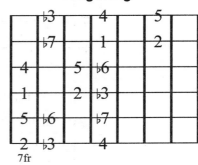

Fingering 6

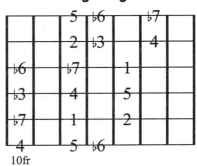

Here are some voicings for the Emin7#5, Amin7#5, and other chords available to us from the intervals unique to the aeolian scale.

Emin7#5
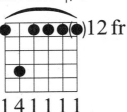
1 4 1 1 1 1

Emin7#5
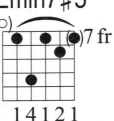
1 4 1 2 1

Emin7#5
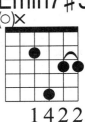
1 4 2 2

Emin7#5
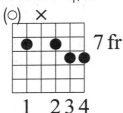
1 2 3 4

Emin7#5
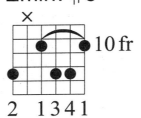
2 1 3 4 1

Emin7#5
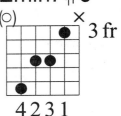
4 2 3 1

Emin7#5
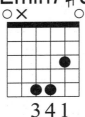
3 4 1

Emin11#5
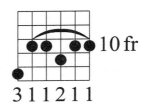
3 1 1 2 1 1

Amin7#5
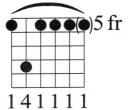
1 4 1 1 1 1

Amin7#5
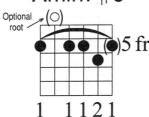
1 1 1 2 1

Fmaj7/A
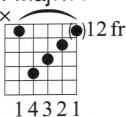
1 4 3 2 1

Amin7#5
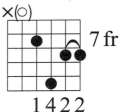
1 4 2 2

Amin7#5
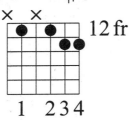
1 2 3 4

Amin7#5
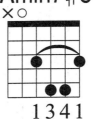
1 3 4 1

Amin7#5
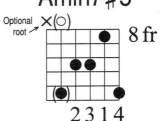
2 3 1 4

Now it's time again to get some more licks under your fingers. Once again the licks will go from easy to hard and will be over the Emin7#5 chord. Have fun!

Example 60

Example 61

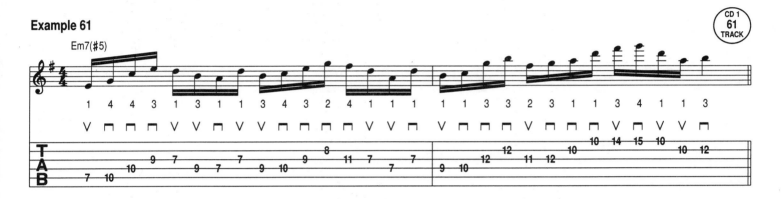

Example 62

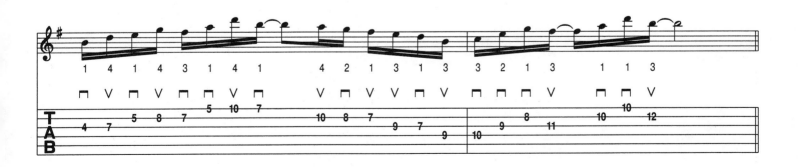

More licks, this time in A aeolian. These licks will go from easy to hard and will all be over the Amin7#5 chord. Play them as accurately as possible.

Example 63

Example 64

Example 65

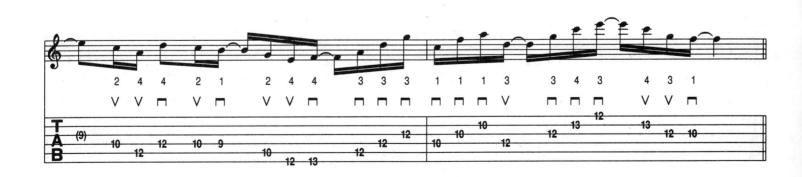

FRANK GAMBALE

More licks. This time we combine the two scales and chords. Study the notes carefully, being sure to read the notes accurately. Good luck!

Example 66

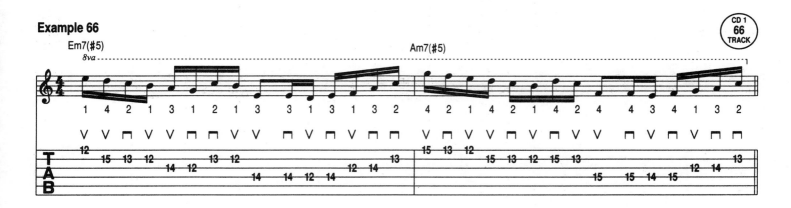

Example 67

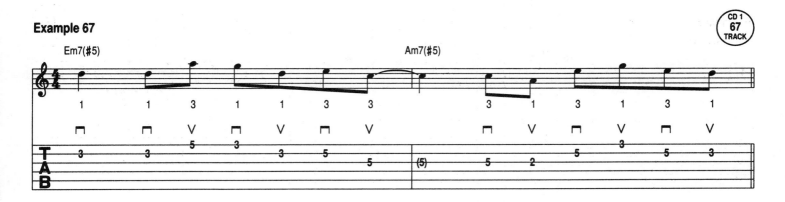

Example 68

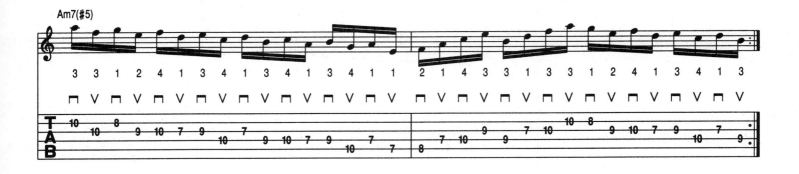

This lesson will demonstrate the use of the aeolian chord in a song context. Once again you'll see mixed chord types. Have fun!

Example 69

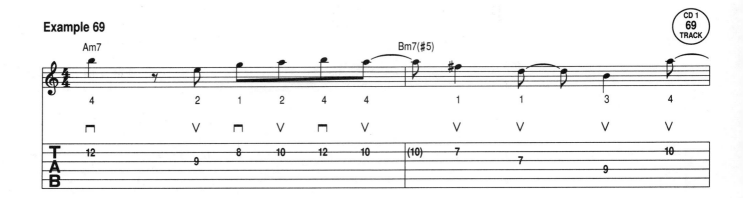

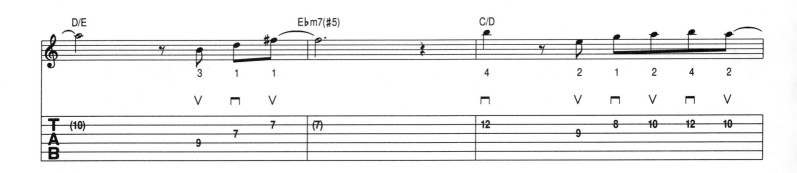

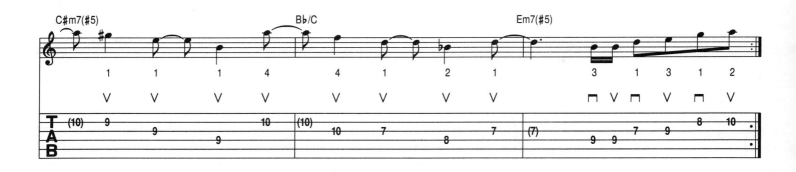

CHAPTER 8

THE LYDIAN ♭7 MODE
(E13#11, E9#11, E13...)

The lydian ♭7 mode is built on the 4th note of a melodic minor scale. E lydian ♭7 would have the same notes as the B melodic minor scale because E is the 4th scale degree of B melodic minor. The notes for B melodic minor: B C# D E F# G# A#. If we begin these notes on E (the 4th note) we have the notes for the E lydian ♭7 scale: E F# G# A# B C# D. To understand the character of the lydian ♭7 scale we must compare these notes to the major scale. If we compare E lydian ♭7 to the notes of E major we have:

E Major:	E	F#	G#	A	B	C#	D#	E	F#	G#	A	B	C#
	1	2	3	4	5	6	7	8	9	10	11	12	13

E Lydian ♭7:	E	F#	G#	**A#**	B	C#	**D**	E	F#	G#	**A#**	B	C#
	1	2	3	**#4**	5	6	**♭7**	8	9	10	**#11**	12	13

Now you can see that the only differences are the #4th and ♭7th in the lydian ♭7 scale. By numbering the degrees we get a scale formula we can use which will be consistent with every lydian ♭7 scale in every key.

Lydian ♭7:
```
1   2   3   #4   5   6   ♭7
   (9)    (#11)    (13)
```

You can see by this scale's interval content that the chords possible from lydian ♭7 are dominant 7 chord characters: E7 (1 3 5 ♭7), E9 (1 3 5 ♭7 9), E13 (1 3 ♭7 13), and E13#11 (1 3 ♭7 #11 13). These are just a few of the possibilities for chords available using the lydian ♭7 interval structure: 1 – 2(9) – 3 – 4(#11) – 5 – 6(13) – ♭7. The most popular lydian ♭7 chords are undoubtedly the 9th, 13th, and 13(#11) chords.

START OF CD 2

Learn all seven scale fingerings for E lydian ♭7. Notice that the scales are written out, numbered in one-octave intervals: 1 2 3 #4 5 6 ♭7. Practice these scale fingerings at a medium tempo.

Fingering 1

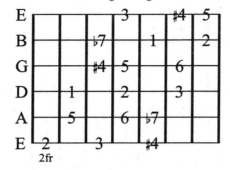

Fingering 3

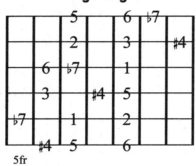

Fingering 5

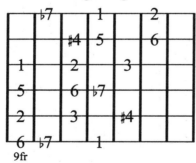

Fingering 7

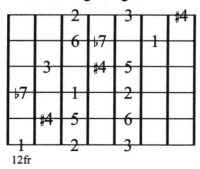

Fingering 2

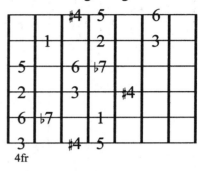

Fingering 4

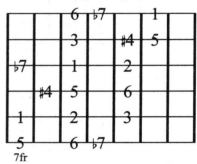

Fingering 6

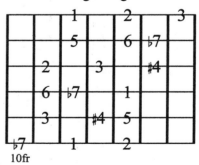

Once you've played all seven fingerings for A lydian ♭7, combine Lessons 1 and 2 by playing the first fingering of E lydian ♭7, then the first fingering of A lydian ♭7, then the second fingering of E lydian ♭7, etc.

Fingering 1

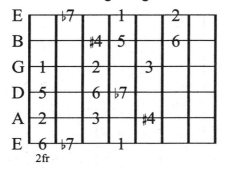

Fingering 2

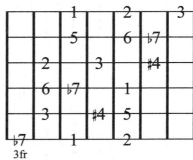

Fingering 3

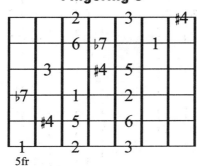

Fingering 4

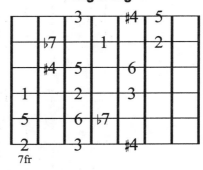

Fingering 5

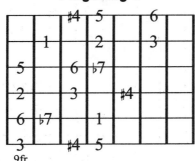

Fingering 6

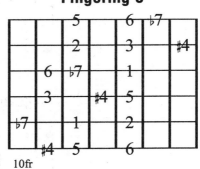

Fingering 7

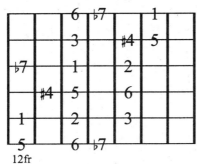

Here are some voicings for the E13#11 , A13#11 , and other chords available to us from the intervals unique to the lydian ♭7 scale.

E13#11
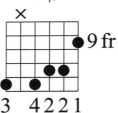
9 fr
3 4 2 2 1

E9#11
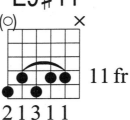
11 fr
2 1 3 1 1

E13#11
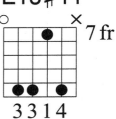
7 fr
3 3 1 4

E13#11
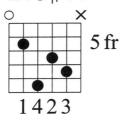
5 fr
1 4 2 3

E13#11
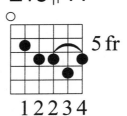
5 fr
1 2 2 3 4

E13
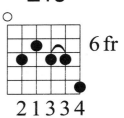
6 fr
2 1 3 3 4

E13
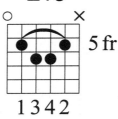
5 fr
1 3 4 2

E13
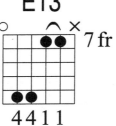
7 fr
4 4 1 1

A13#11
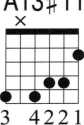
3 4 2 2 1

A13#11
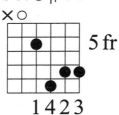
5 fr
1 4 2 3

A9#11
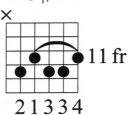
11 fr
2 1 3 3 4

A9#11
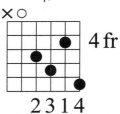
4 fr
2 3 1 4

A13#11
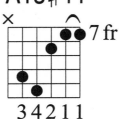
7 fr
3 4 2 1 1

A13
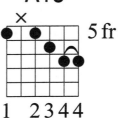
5 fr
1 2 3 4 4

A13
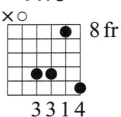
8 fr
3 3 1 4

FRANK GAMBALE

LICKS IN E LYDIAN ♭7

Now it's time again to get some more licks under your fingers. These licks will go
from easy to hard and will be over the E9 chord. Have fun!

Example 70

Example 71

Example 72

IMPROVISING MADE EASIER

More licks, this time in A lydian ♭7. These licks will go from easy to hard and will all be over the A13 chord. Play them as accurately as possible.

Example 73

Example 74

Example 75

FRANK GAMBALE

More licks. This time we combine the two scales and chords. Study the notes carefully, being sure to read the notes accurately. Good luck!

Example 76

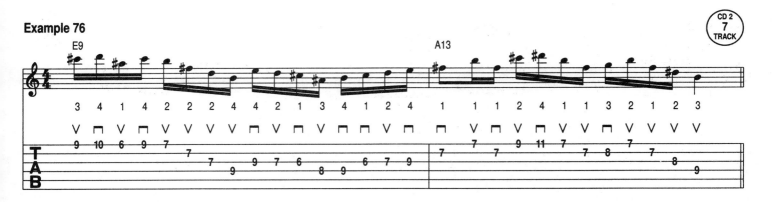

Example 77

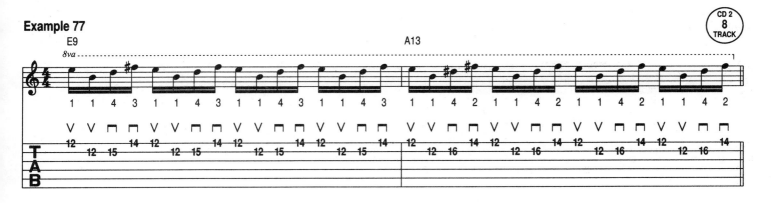

Example 78

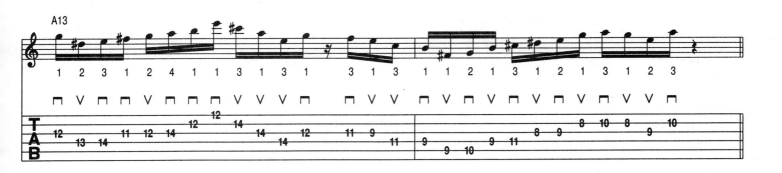

This lesson will demonstrate the use of the lydian ♭7 chord in a song context. Once again you'll see mixed chord types. Have fun!

Example 79

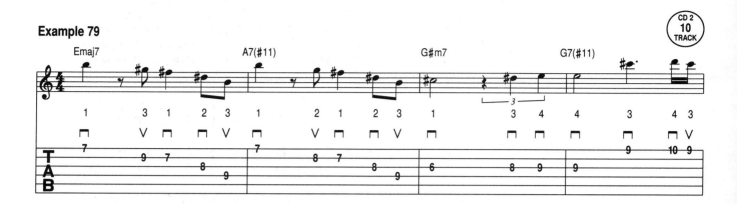

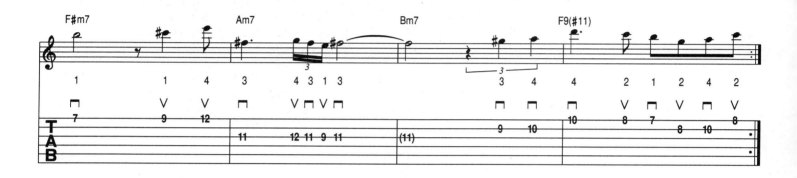

FRANK GAMBALE

CHAPTER 9

THE SUPER LOCRIAN MODE
(E7#9, E7#5#9, E7♭5#9...)

A super locrian scale is built on the 7th note of a melodic minor scale. E super locrian would have the same notes as the F melodic minor scale because E is the 7th scale degree of F melodic minor. The notes of F melodic minor = F G A♭ B♭ C D E. If we begin these notes on E (the 7th note) we have the notes for the E super locrian scale: E F G A♭ B♭ C D. To understand the character of the super locrian scale we must compare these notes to the major scale. If we compare E super locrian to the notes of E major we have:

E Major:	E	F#	G#	A	B	C#	D#	E	F#	G#	A	B	C#
	1	2	3	4	5	6	7	8	9	10	11	12	13

E Super Locrian:	E	F	G	G#	B♭	C	D	E	F	G	G#	B♭	C
	1	♭2	♭3	3	♭5	#5	♭7	8	♭9	#9	10	#11	♭13

Now you can see that the differences are that the 2nd, 3rd, 4th, 5th, 6th, and 7th are flat (lowered 1/2 step) in the super locrian scale. This scale has some peculiar intervals which I'd like to take a moment to explain. The ♭2 and ♭3 are the same notes as the ♭9 and #9, the latter of which you'll see occurring the most in chord symbols. You've no doubt seen a 7(♭9) chord more often than a 7(add ♭2). So remember that point. Another thing to remember is that this scale also has a ♭5 and ♭6. The ♭6 should be regarded as a #5 which is the way you'll see it appear the most. You'll never see a m7 ♭6 chord. So be aware of this point also. One more thing: this scale also has a natural 3rd as well as a ♭3rd. In a 7(#9) chord both notes are used, but remember that the ♭3 in this case is regarded as a #9. The formula for this chord is 1 3 ♭7 #9. By numbering the degrees we get a scale formula we can use which will be consistent with every super locrian scale in every key.

Super Locrian:	1	♭2	♭3	3	♭5	#5	♭7
		(♭9)			(#11)		(♭13)

You can see by this scale's interval content that the chords possible from super locrian are dominant 7 chords with a #5 and/or ♭5, #9 and/or ♭9 (and any combination thereof): E7#9 (1 3 ♭7 #9), E7♭9 (1 3 ♭7 ♭9), and E7#5♭9 (1 3 #5 ♭7 ♭9). These are just a few of the possibilities for chords available using the super locrian interval structure: 1 ♭2(♭9) ♭3 ♭4(3) ♭5 ♭6(♭13) ♭7. The most popular super locrian chord is undoubtedly the 7(#9).

Learn all seven scale fingerings for E super locrian. Notice that the scales are written out, numbered in one-octave intervals: 1 ♭2 ♭3 3(♭4) ♭5 ♯5(♭6) ♭7. Practice these scale fingerings at a medium tempo, then gradually play them faster.

Fingering 1

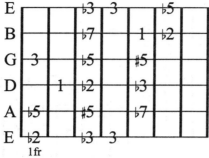

Fingering 2

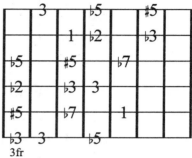

Fingering 3

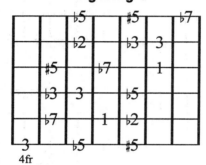

Fingering 4

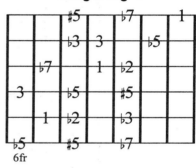

Fingering 5

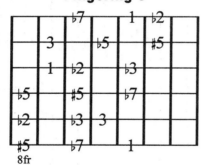

Fingering 6

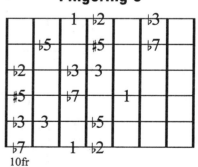

Fingering 7

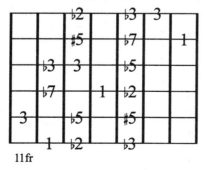

Once you've played all seven fingerings for A super locrian, combine Lessons 1 and 2 by playing the first fingering of E super locrian, then the first fingering of A super locrian, then the second fingering of E super locrian, etc.

Fingering 1

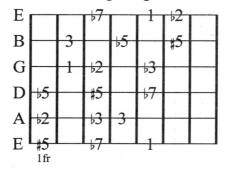

Fingering 3

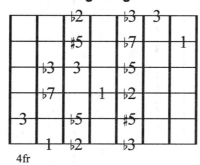

Fingering 5

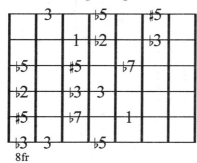

Fingering 7

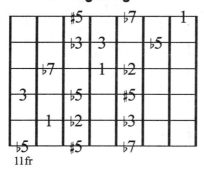

Fingering 2

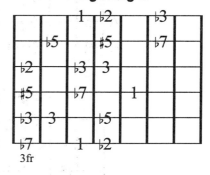

Fingering 4

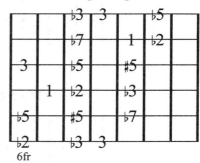

Fingering 6

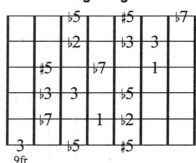

Here are some voicings for the E7♯9, A7♯9, and other chords available to us from the intervals unique to the super locrian scale.

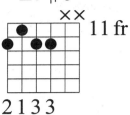

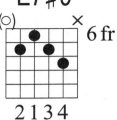

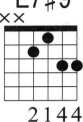

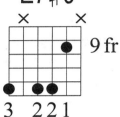

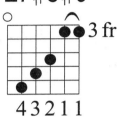

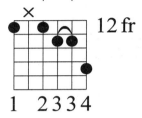

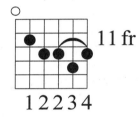

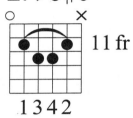

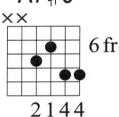

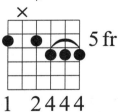

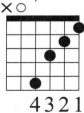

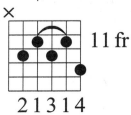

Now it's time to get some more licks under your fingers. Once again the licks will go from easy to hard and will be over the E7#9 chord. Have fun!

Example 80

CD 2
11
TRACK

Example 81

CD 2
12
TRACK

Example 82

CD 2
13
TRACK

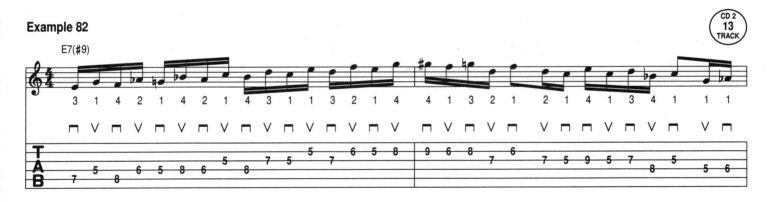

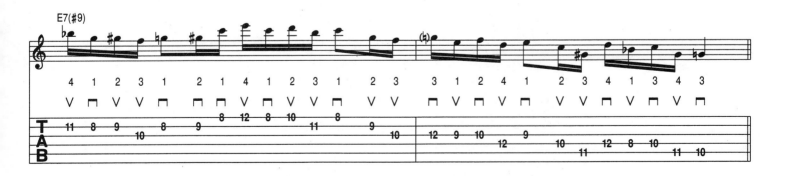

More licks, this time in A super locrian. These licks will go from easy to hard and will all be over the A7#9 chord. Play them as accurately as possible.

Example 83

CD 2 14 TRACK

Example 84

CD 2 15 TRACK

Example 85

CD 2 16 TRACK

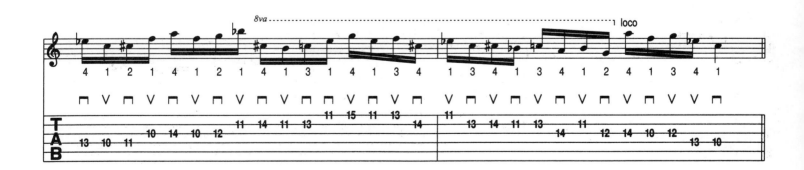

More licks. This time we combine the two scales and chords. Study the notes carefully, being sure to read the notes accurately. Good luck!

Example 86

Example 87

Example 88

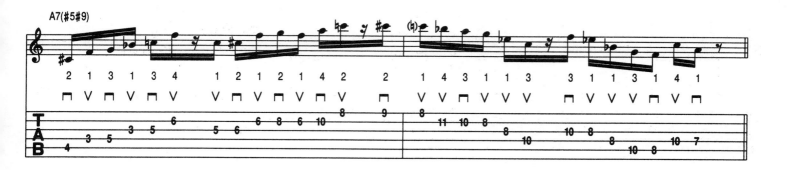

This lesson will demonstrate the use of the super locrian chord in a song context.
Once again you'll see mixed chord types. Have fun!

Example 89

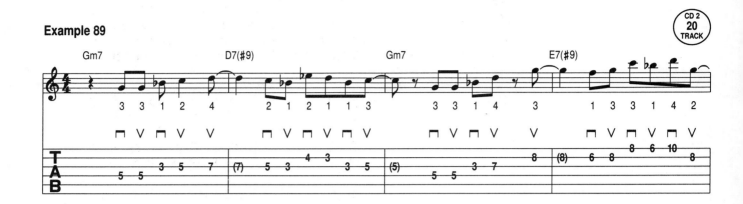

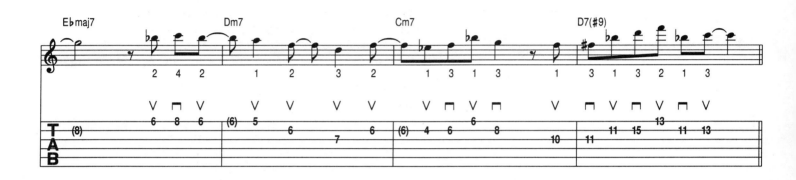

CHAPTER 10

THE HALF-WHOLE DIMINISHED SCALE
(E13♭9, E13♭9♯11, E7♯9...)

A half-whole diminished scale is a completely symmetrical scale constructed from the note arrangement of 1/2 step, then whole step, then 1/2 step, etc. E half-whole diminished would have the notes E F G G♯ A♯ B C♯ D. To understand the character of the half-whole diminished scale we must compare these notes to the major scale. If we compare E half-whole diminished to the notes of the E major scale we have:

E Major:	E	F♯	G♯		A	B	C♯	D♯	E	F♯		G♯	A	B	C♯
	1	2	3		4	5	6	7	8	9		10	11	12	13

E half-whole diminished:	E	**F**	**G**	G♯	**A♯**	B	C♯	**D**	E	**F**	**G**	G♯	**A♯**	B	C♯
	1	♭**2**	♭**3**	3	♯**4**	5	6	♭**7**	8	♭**9**	♯**9**	10	♯**11**	12	13

Now you can see that the differences are the ♭2nd, ♭3rd, ♯4th, and ♭7th in the half-whole diminished scale. This scale has some peculiar intervals which I'd like to take a moment to explain. The ♭2 is the same note as the ♭9 and the ♭3 is the same as the ♯9 (see below), the latter of which (♭9 and ♯9) you'll see occurring the most in chord symbols. This scale has a natural 3rd as well as a ♭3rd. In a 7(♯9) chord both notes are used, but remember that the ♭3 is regarded as a ♯9. The formula for this chord is 1 3 ♭7 ♯9. If we number the degrees we get a scale formula we can use which will be consistent with every half-whole diminished scale in every key.

1/2-Whole Diminished:	1	♭2	♯2/♭3	3	♯4/♭5	5	6	♭7
		(♭9)	(♯9)		(♯11)		(13)	

You can see by this scale's interval content that the chords possible from half-whole diminished are dominant 7 chords with a ♯9 and/or ♭9, and a natural 6th (usually shown in the chord as a 13th): E13♭9 (1 3 ♭7 ♭9 13), E7♭9 (1 3 ♭7 ♭9), and E7♭5♭9 (1 3 ♭5 ♭7 ♭9). These are just some of the possibilities for chords available using the half-whole diminished interval structure: 1 ♭2(♭9) ♯2/♭3(♯9) 3 ♯4/♭5(♯11) 5 6(13) ♭7. The most popular half-whole diminished chord is undoubtedly the 13(♭9).

Learn all four scale fingerings for E half-whole diminished. Notice that the scales are written out, numbered in one-octave intervals: 1 ♭2 ♭3(♯2) 3 ♭5(♯4) 5 6 ♭7. Practice these scale fingerings at a medium tempo, then gradually play them faster.

Fingering 1

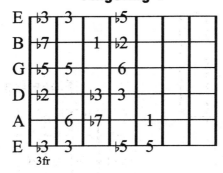

Fingering 2

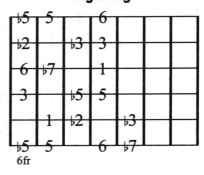

Fingering 3

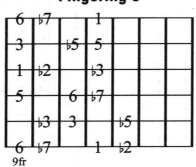

Fingering 4

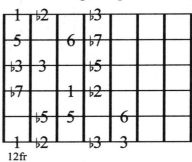

Once you've played all four fingerings for A half-whole diminished, combine Lessons 1 and 2 by playing the first fingering of E half-whole diminished, then the first fingering of A half-whole diminished, then the second fingering of E half-whole diminished, etc.

Fingering 1

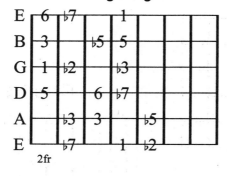

Fingering 3

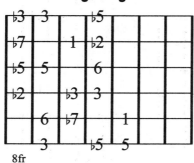

Fingering 2

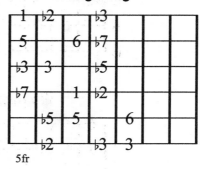

Fingering 4

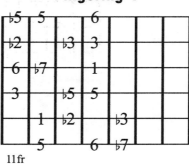

CHORD VOICINGS FOR E13♭9, A13♭9, AND OTHER HALF-WHOLE DIMINISHED CHORDS

Here are some voicings for the E13♭9, A13♭9, and other chords available to us from the intervals unique to the half-whole diminished scale.

E13♭9

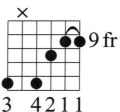

9 fr

3 4 2 1 1

E13♭9♯11
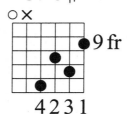

9 fr

4 2 3 1

E13♯9
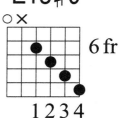

6 fr

1 2 3 4

E13♭9
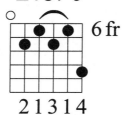

6 fr

2 1 3 1 4

E13♭9
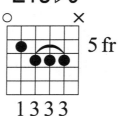

5 fr

1 3 3 3

E7♯9
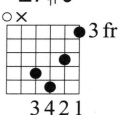

3 fr

3 4 2 1

A13♭9
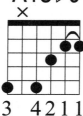

3 4 2 1 1

A13♭9♯11
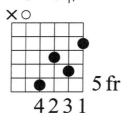

5 fr

4 2 3 1

A13♯9
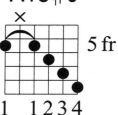

5 fr

1 1 2 3 4

A13♭9
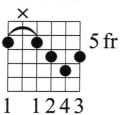

5 fr

1 1 2 4 3

A7♯9
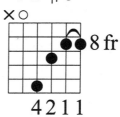

8 fr

4 2 1 1

A13♯9
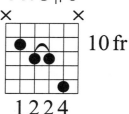

10 fr

1 2 2 4

A13♭9
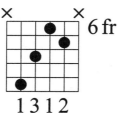

6 fr

1 3 1 2

A13♭9
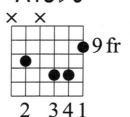

9 fr

2 3 4 1

LICKS IN E HALF-WHOLE DIMINISHED

Now it's time again for some more licks. These licks will go from easy to hard and will be over the E13♭9#11 chord. Have fun!

Example 90

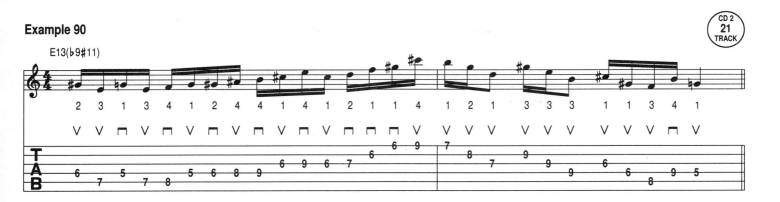

Example 91

Example 92

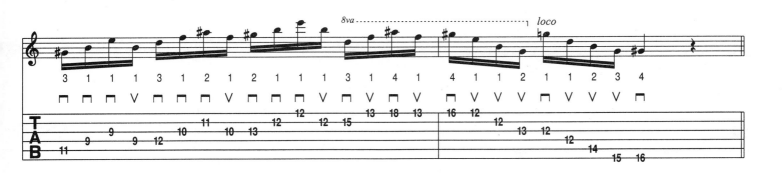

More licks, this time in A half-whole diminished. These licks will go from easy to hard and will all be over the A13♭9♯11 chord. Play them as accurately as possible.

Example 93

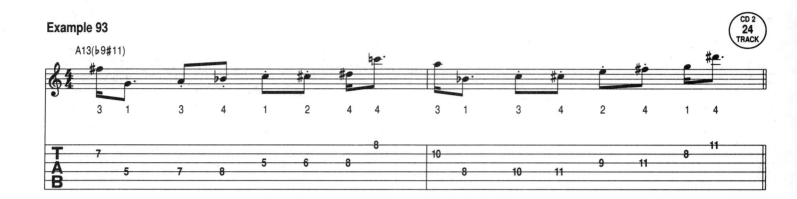

Example 94

Example 95

More licks. This time we combine the two scales and chords. Study the notes carefully, being sure to read the notes accurately. Good luck!

Example 96

Example 97

Example 98

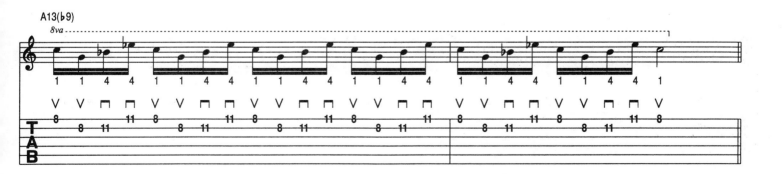

This lesson will demonstrate the use of the half-whole diminished chord in a song context. Once again you'll see mixed chord types. Have fun!

Example 99

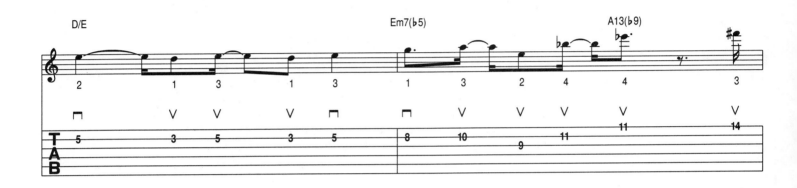

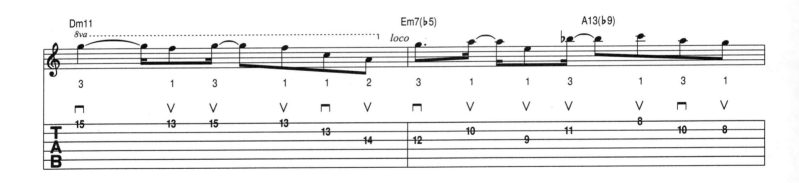

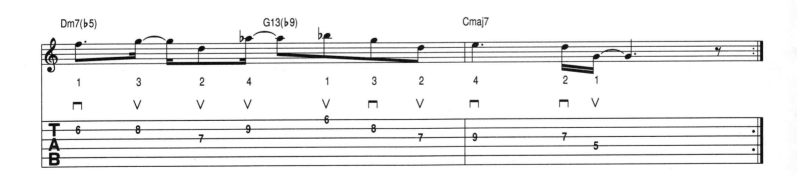

CHAPTER 11

THE PHRYGIAN MAJOR MODE
(E(♭9), Esus(♭9), Gmin⁶₉/A...)

The phrygian major scale is built on the 5th note of a harmonic minor scale. The scale formula for harmonic minor is: 1 2 ♭3 4 5 ♭6 7. E phrygian major would have the same notes as A harmonic minor because E is the 5th scale degree of A harmonic minor. The notes of A harmonic minor are A B C D E F G♯, so the notes for E phrygian major would be E F G♯ A B C D. To understand the character of the phrygian major scale we must compare these notes to the major scale. If we compare E phrygian major to the notes of E major we have:

E Major:	E	F♯	G♯	A	B	C♯	D♯	E	F♯	G♯	A	B	C♯
	1	2	3	4	5	6	7	8	9	10	11	12	13

E Phrygian Major:	E	**F**	G♯	A	B	**C**	**D**	E	**F**	G♯	A	B	**C**
	1	**♭2**	3	4	5	**♭6**	**♭7**	8	**♭9**	10	11	12	**♭13**

Now you can see that the only differences are the ♭2nd, ♭6th, and ♭7th in the phrygian major scale. By numbering the degrees we get a scale formula we can use which will be consistent with every phrygian major scale in every key.

Phrygian Major:	1	♭2	3	4	5	♭6	♭7
		(♭9)		(11)		(♭13)	

You can see by this scale's interval content that the chords possible from phrygian major are dominant 7 chords with a ♭9 and a ♯5th and/or natural 5th: E(♭9) (1 3 5 ♭9), and E7♭9 (1 3 ♭7 ♭9). These are just a few of the possibilities for chords available using the phrygian major interval structure: 1 ♭2(♭9) 3 4(11) 5 ♭6(♭13) ♭7. The most popular phrygian major chord is undoubtedly the major (♭9) or 7(♭9).

Learn all seven scale fingerings for E phrygian major. You'll notice that the scales are written out, numbered in one-octave intervals: 1 ♭2 3 4 5 ♭6 ♭7. Practice these scale fingerings at a medium tempo, then gradually play them faster.

Fingering 1

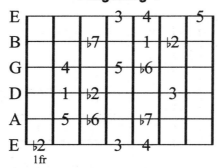

Fingering 2

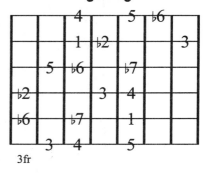

Fingering 3

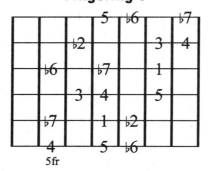

Fingering 4

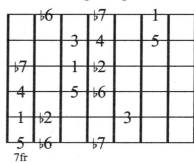

Fingering 5

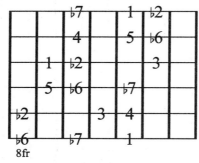

Fingering 6

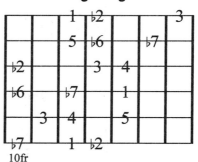

Fingering 7

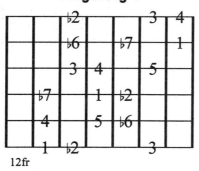

SCALE FINGERINGS FOR A PHRYGIAN MAJOR

Once you've played all seven fingerings for A phrygian major, combine Lessons 1 and 2 by playing the first fingering of E phrygian major, then the first fingering of A phrygian major, then the second fingering of E phrygian major, etc.

Fingering 1
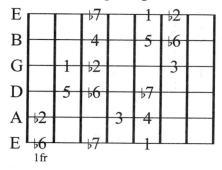

Fingering 2
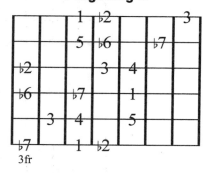

Fingering 3
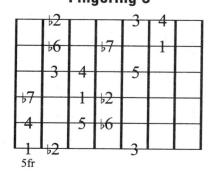

Fingering 4
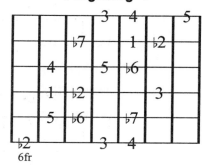

Fingering 5
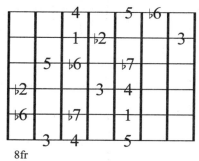

Fingering 6
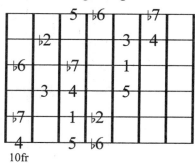

Fingering 7
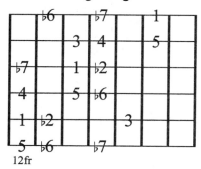

CHORD VOICINGS FOR
E AND A PHRYGIAN MAJOR CHORDS

Here are some voicings for the E(♭9), A(♭9), and other chords available to us from the intervals unique to the phrygian major scale.

E(♭9)

2 3 1

Esus4(♭9)

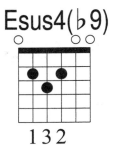

1 3 2

E(♭9)

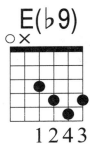

1 2 4 3

E(♭9)

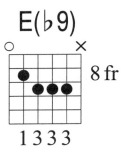

8 fr

1 3 3 3

E7♭9

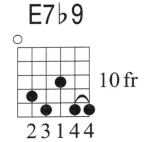

10 fr

2 3 1 4 4

E7sus4(♭9)

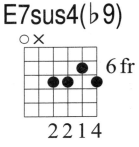

6 fr

2 2 1 4

A(♭9)

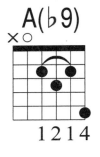

1 2 1 4

A(♭9)

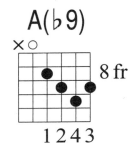

8 fr

1 2 4 3

A(♭9)

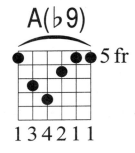

5 fr

1 3 4 2 1 1

A(♭9)

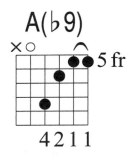

5 fr

4 2 1 1

A(♭9)

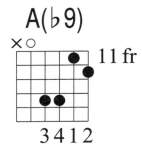

11 fr

3 4 1 2

A7♭9

3 2 1 4

A7♭9

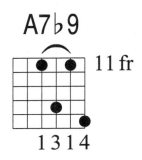

11 fr

1 3 1 4

A7♭9

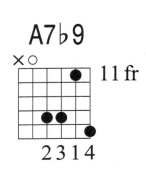

11 fr

2 3 1 4

Gmin⁶/₉/A

2 3 1 4 4

Now it's time again for some more licks. These licks will go from easy to hard and will be over the E7♭9 chord. Have fun!

Example 100

Example 101

Example 102

More licks, this time in A phrygian major. These licks will go from easy to hard and will all be over the A7♭9 chord. Play them as accurately as possible.

Example 103

Example 104

Example 105

More licks. This time we combine the two scales and chords. Study the notes carefully, being sure to read the notes accurately. Good luck!

Example 106

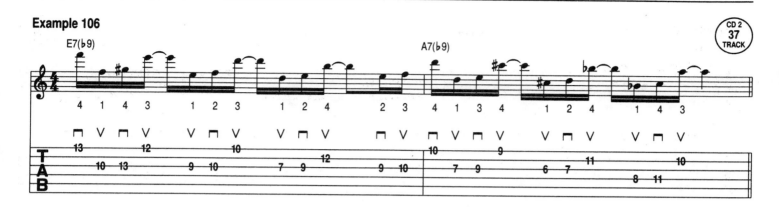

Example 107

Example 108

SONG EXAMPLE USING
HARMONIC MINOR V(5) CHORDS

This lesson will demonstrate the use of the phrygian major chord in a song context. Once again you'll see mixed chord types. Have fun!

Example 109

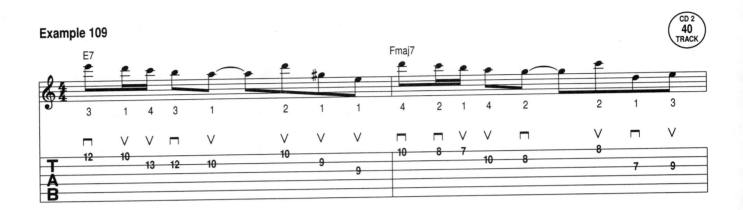

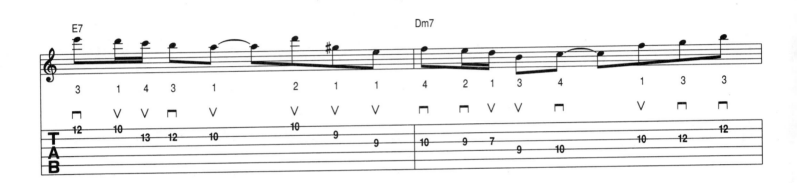

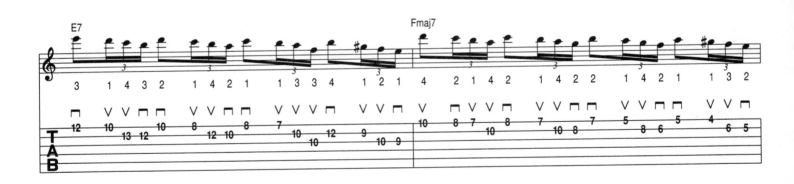

FRANK GAMBALE

CHAPTER 12

THE AEOLIAN ♭5 SCALE
(Emin11♭5, Emin♭5, Amin11♭5...)

The aeolian ♭5 mode is built on the 6th note of a melodic minor scale. E aeolian ♭5 would have the same notes as the G melodic minor scale because E is the 6th scale degree of G melodic minor. The notes of G melodic minor = G A B♭ C D E F#. If we begin these notes on E we have the E aeolian ♭5 scale (E F# G A B♭ C D). To understand the character of the aeolian ♭5 scale we must compare these notes to the major scale. If we compare E aeolian ♭5 to the notes of the E major scale we have:

E Major:	E	F#	G#	A	B	C#	D#	E	F#	G#	A	B	C#
	1	2	3	4	5	6	7	8	9	10	11	12	13

E Aeolian ♭5:	E	F#	**G**	A	**B♭**	**C**	**D**	E	F#	**G**	A	**B♭**	**C**
	1	2	**♭3**	4	**♭5**	**♭6**	**♭7**	8	9	**♭10**	11	**#11**	**♭13**

Now you can see that the differences are the ♭3rd, ♭5th, ♭6th, and ♭7th in the aeolian ♭5 scale. By numbering the degrees we get a scale formula we can use which will be consistent with every aeolian ♭5 scale in every key.

Aeolian ♭5:	1	2	♭3	4	♭5	♭6	♭7
		(9)		(11)		(♭13)	

You can see by this scale's interval content that the chords possible from aeolian ♭5 are minor 7(♭5) chords with a natural 9: Emin9♭5 (1 ♭3 ♭5 ♭7 ♭9) and Emin11♭5 (1 ♭3 ♭5 ♭9 9 11). These are just a few of the possibilities for chords available using the aeolian ♭5 interval structure: 1 2(9) ♭3 4(11) ♭5 ♭6(♭13) ♭7. The most popular aeolian ♭5 chord is undoubtedly the minor 9(♭5).

Learn all seven scale fingerings for E aeolian ♭5. You'll notice that the scales are written out, numbered in one-octave intervals: 1 2 ♭3 4 ♭5 ♭6 ♭7. Practice these scale fingerings at a medium tempo, then gradually play them faster.

Fingering 1

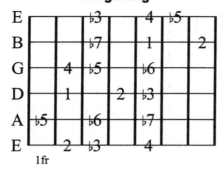

Fingering 2

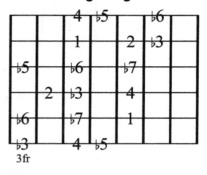

Fingering 3

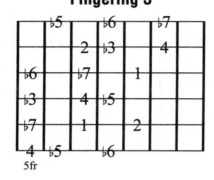

Fingering 4

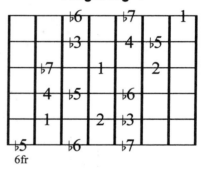

Fingering 5

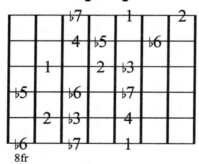

Fingering 6

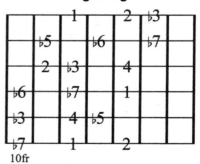

Fingering 7

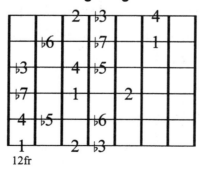

Once you've played all seven fingerings for A aeolian ♭5, combine Lessons 1 and 2 by playing the first fingering of E aeolian ♭5, then the first fingering of A aeolian ♭5, then the second fingering of E aeolian ♭5, etc.

Fingering 1

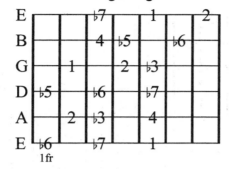

Fingering 2

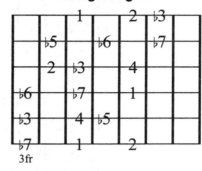

Fingering 3

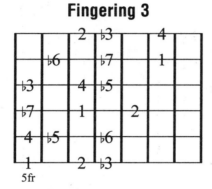

Fingering 4

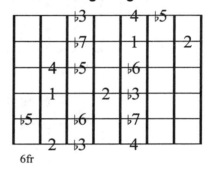

Fingering 5

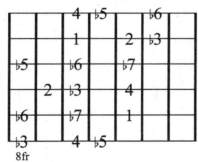

Fingering 6

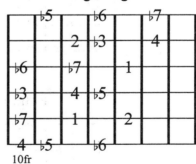

Fingering 7

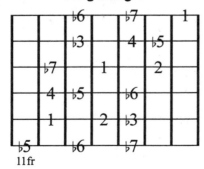

Here are some voicings for the Emin9♭5, Amin9♭5, and other chords available to us from the intervals unique to the aeolian ♭5 scale.

Emin11♭5
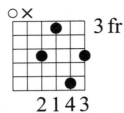

Emin9♭5
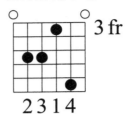

Emin9♭5
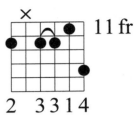

Emin11♭5
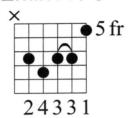

Emin9♭5
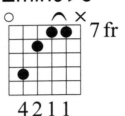

Emin11♭5
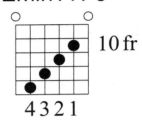

Emin11♭5
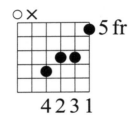

Emin9♭5
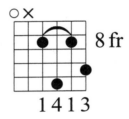

Amin11♭5
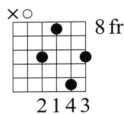

Amin9♭5
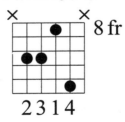

Amin9♭5
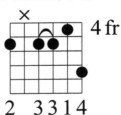

Amin11♭5
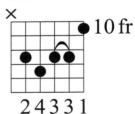

Amin9♭5
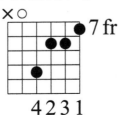

Amin11♭5
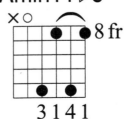

Amin11♭5
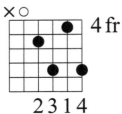

FRANK GAMBALE

Now it's time again for some more licks. These licks will go from easy to hard and will be over the Emin9♭5 chord. Have fun!

Example 110

Example 111

Example 112

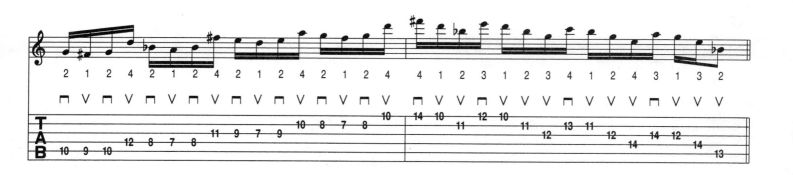

LICKS IN A AEOLIAN ♭5

More licks, this time in A aeolian ♭5. These licks will go from easy to hard and will all be over the Amin9♭5 chord. Play them as accurately as possible.

Example 113

CD 2 44 TRACK

Example 114

CD 2 45 TRACK

Example 115

CD 2 46 TRACK

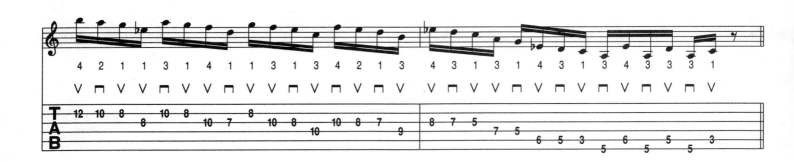

FRANK GAMBALE

COMBINATION LICKS IN E AND A AEOLIAN ♭5

More licks. This time we combine the two scales and chords. Study the notes carefully, being sure to read the notes accurately. Good luck!

Example 116

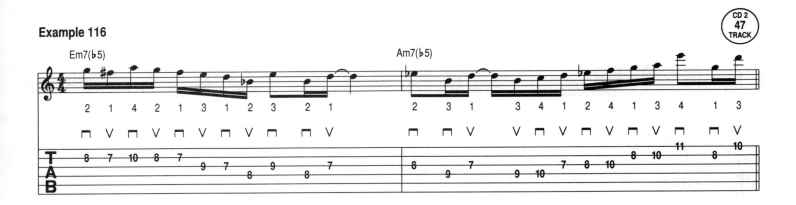

Example 117

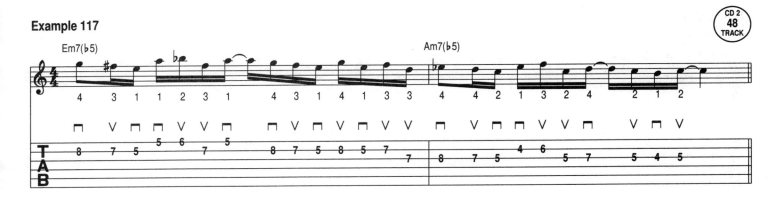

Example 118

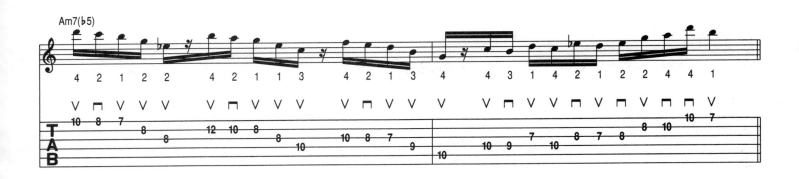

This lesson will demonstrate the use of the aeolian ♭5 chord in a song context.
Once again you'll see mixed chord types. Have fun!

Example 119

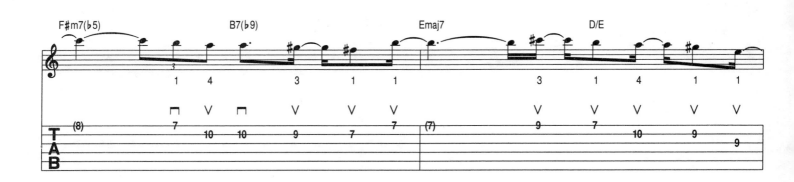

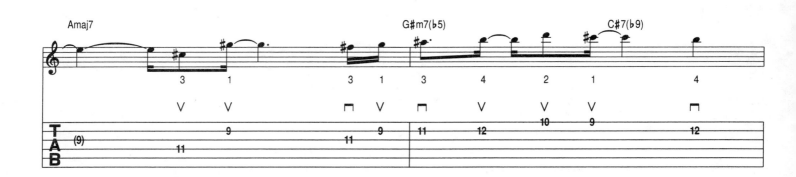

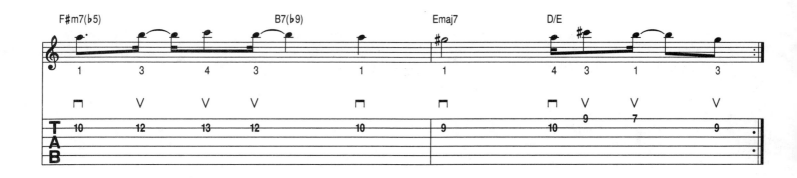

FRANK GAMBALE

In this last section I wrote a pretty challenging piece entitled, "Modalawn," which incorporates all that we have learned throughout the entire Improvising Course.

If you made it this far you must be ripping up that fretboard by now! There's a great deal of information in this book to digest, but if you follow the procedure of inputting each lesson in each of the chapters, you can really accelerate as a player and overcome those ruts that we fall into from not knowing exactly what to practice or which direction to go in to become a better player. Stick with this intense improvisational course and I guarantee you'll come out ahead of the pack.

Good luck and happy picking to all!

Frank Gambale

MODALAWN

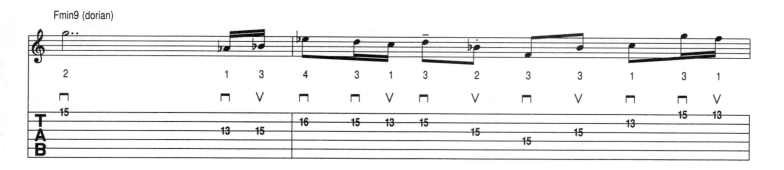

Cmaj9 (major)

Dbmaj7b5/C (C phrygian)

B/F (F locrian)

Emaj9 (E lydian)

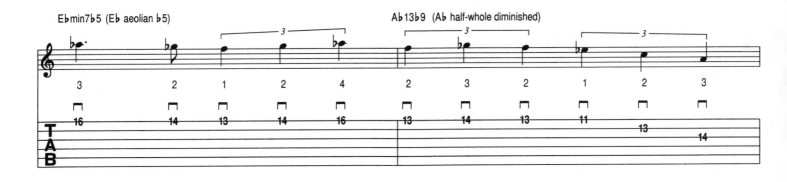

Ebmin7b5 (Eb aeolian b5)   Ab13b9 (Ab half-whole diminished)

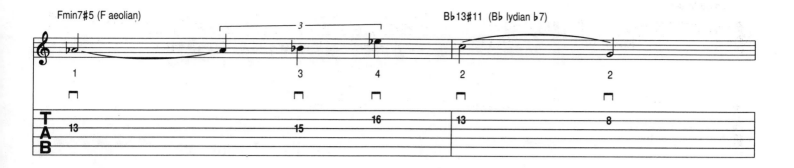

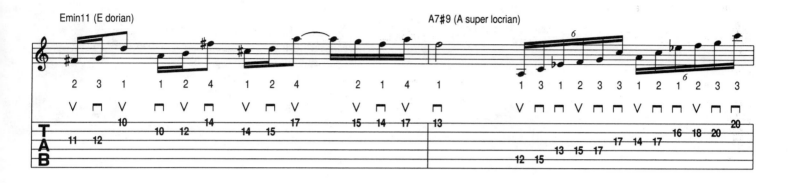

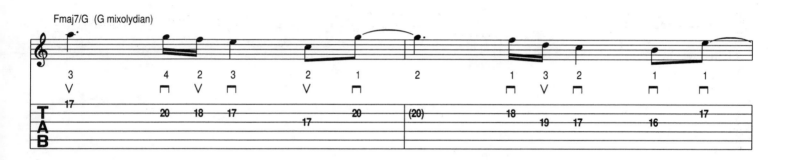

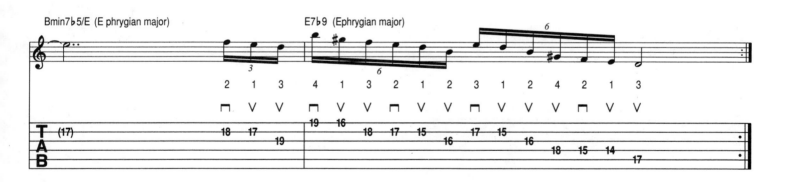

ALSO AVAILABLE FROM FRANK GAMBALE AND WARNER BROS. PUBLICATIONS

BOOKS—

The Frank Gambale Technique Book 1

The essential soloing theory course for all guitarists. This method is structured around six basic chordal types approached five ways. Book 1 covers the first four chordal types and includes a 60-minute recording.

Book and cassette MMBK0002AT $24.95
Book and CD MMBK0002CD $26.95

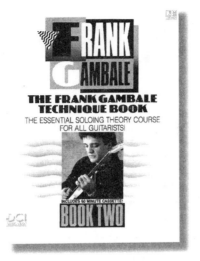

The Frank Gambale Technique Book 2

This method looks at soloing over chordal harmonies. It demonstrates how to use simple musical materials to create sophisticated solo. Includes a 70-minute recording.

Book and cassette MMBK0003AT $24.95
Book and CD MMBK0003CD $26.95

Guitar Lessons with the Greats

John Abercrombie, Kevin Eubanks, Frank Gambale, Scott Henderson, Steve Lukather, Mike Stern
In Guitar Lessons with the Greats, six major artists known for their innovative contributions to contemporary jazz, rock and fusion guitar share the vast knowledge and experience that keeps them on the cutting edge of the music world.

Book and cassette MMBK0039AT $21.95
Book and CD MMBK0039CD $24.95

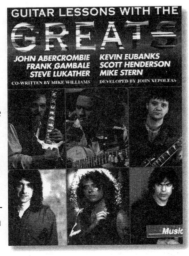

VIDEOS—

Chop Builder: The Ultimate Guitar Workout

Keep your chops in shape! This exciting and challenging motivational video will inspire you to practice. Gambale's routine is designed to increase speed and dexterity while improving music theory and fretboard knowledge. **With booklet.   REH859 $49.95**

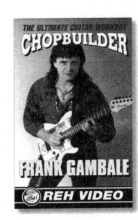

Modes: No More Mystery

This video is a clear and easy-to-understand guide to using modes in soloing. Gambale takes a subject that guitarists often find confusing and explains it in simple terms. All seven major modes are covered and demonstrated with some extraordinary solo work.
VHO100 $49.95

Monster Licks and Speed Picking

This video details Gambale's innovative speed/sweep picking technique and presents a method for developing "monster licks." He demonstrates his picking technique in the context of scales, pentatonics, arpeggios and triad examples, playing each slowly and then at lightning speed. Booklet included.
VHO41 $49.95

Available at your local music retailer or call toll free 1-800-628-1528 ext. 215/214